Wind Loggers

All rights reserved. No part of this book shall be reproduced or transmitted in any form or by any means, electronic, mechanical, magnetic, photographic including photocopying, recording or by any information storage and retrieval system, without prior written permission of the publisher. No patent liability is assumed with respect to the use of the information contained herein. Although every precaution has been taken in the preparation of this book, the publisher and author assume no responsibility for errors or omissions. Neither is any liability assumed for damages resulting from the use of the information contained herein.

Stories previously published:

Autorotate Magazine:
"When Turbines Explode…"
"Adios Gearbox, and Down She Goes!"
"Good-bye Drive Shaft, Hello Trees!"
"Deadeye Lyle and the Sons of the Code Talkers"
"Returning to Mother Earth Without Power"
"Parlez Vous Long-line?"
"Flying the DynaFlight-SeisBag"
"That…was No Mechanic!"
"Miss America Visits the 'Nam"

Aviation International News:
"Helicopter Lightning!"

Aviation Maintenance:
"A Boot Full of Trouble"
"Helicopter Logging and the Ideal Field Mechanic"
"When Igor Went Thru the Rotors…"
"And One That Got Away!"
"Big Al's 'Head's Up' Award!"

HelicopterMonthly.com:
"Look Boss, No Skids!"
"Logs That Punish!"
"Plan 'B' From Outer Montana"
"Flying the Ultra-Ripe, Blue Plastic Outhouse!"

Wind Loggers

[signed] DAWingo 1-16-'19

Dorcey Alan Wingo
"Captain Methane"

New Revised 2015 Edition

With Expanded Helicopter Loggers Glossary

Copyright © 2015 by Dorcey Alan Wingo.
Front cover photo by the late Douglas D. Bosworth.
Back cover photo by David R. Busse.

Library of Congress Control Number:		2015901078
ISBN:	Hardcover	978-1-5035-3685-2
	Softcover	978-1-5035-3687-6
	eBook	978-1-5035-3686-9

All rights reserved. No part of this book may be reproduced or transmitted in any form or by any means, electronic or mechanical, including photocopying, recording, or by any information storage and retrieval system, without permission in writing from the copyright owner.

Any people depicted in stock imagery provided by Thinkstock are models, and such images are being used for illustrative purposes only.
Certain stock imagery © Thinkstock.

Print information available on the last page.

Rev. date: 05/29/2015

To order additional copies of this book, contact:
Xlibris
1-888-795-4274
www.Xlibris.com
Orders@Xlibris.com
701318

Contents

Editor's Note: 7
Acknowledgments 9

Introduction: The T-Factor! 11
Mark Meets Bildo 14
Parlez Vous Long-Line? 20
Adios, Gearbox, And Down She Goes! 23
Helicopter Logging And The Ideal Field Mechanic 30
Logs That Punish! 35
That…Was No Mechanic! 39
When Rotors Depart… 45
A Boot Full Of Trouble! 49
Big Al's "Heads-Up" Award! 52
When Turbines Explode! 57
Bigger Is Better, Eh? 63
Goodbye Drive Shaft, Hello Trees! 71
Plan "B" From Outer Montana 75
Dead-Eye Lyle And The Sons Of The Code Talkers 81
Helicopter Lightning! 89
Flying the DynaFlight-Seisbag 93
Returning To Mother… 97
Miss America Visits The 'Nam 103
Rat Wars! 106
Never Fly With Your Brother In A Dive Bomber! 110
Shoot-Out At The Corner Bar! 113
You The Pilot? 116
Unique McPeak and the Classic Stall 121

Flying The Ultra-Ripe, Blue Plastic Outhouse 125
To Catch A Smokejumper 131
Blue Guys...139
Trouble At Dead Horse Pass 143
And One That Got Away..150

Helicopter Loggers' Glossary 153

Editor's Note:

When I first met Dorcey Wingo, he was doing me a huge favor, consenting to an interview about a sensitive subject. All I knew about Dorcey was what my editor had told me when he gave me the story assignment: "Why don't you go down to southern California and see if you can interview that Wingo fella who was involved in that 'Twilight Zone' movie crash. I heard that his trial just finished."

I tracked Dorcey down and to my surprise, he agreed to the interview. Before he could change his mind, I sped down south from where I lived in Oakland in my efficient Honda CRX HF (50+ mpg!) and met Dorcey where he was working at the time, the Western Helicopters hangar at Rialto Airport east of Los Angeles.

We spent the day talking; mostly Dorcey spoke, recounting his adventures as a helicopter pilot, how he had been christened the "Gringo Wingo from Chilpancingo" on one job in southern Mexico, how he met his lovely wife Lourdes, with whom we took a break for lunch, and then, finally, the tragic "Twilight Zone" accident, which irretrievably altered Dorcey's life and ended his attraction to film work.

Life is funny. Where you are at any given moment is a direct result of every previous moment. If the tragedy, and the comedy, hadn't happened just the way they did, you probably wouldn't be reading this.

Since the tragedy, Dorcey has lived the life of adventure as a helicopter logging pilot. Between these risky adventures—probably the most dangerous flying he's done—except for hauling troops in and out of combat zones in Vietnam—he has documented his thoughts and feelings, captured the flavor of his many adventures, and turned out a highly entertaining read that pulls the reader into a world of hair-raising antics, dangerous flying assignments, and crazy but hard working, fun-loving people.

Dorcey Wingo brings to life a world that most of us will never experience, the intense life of a Wind Logger. Or as he puts it so eloquently, "big fat rotor blades banging out tunes from Rotor Heaven."

Matt Thurber, Marina del Rey, California 2015

Acknowledgments

What you hold in your hands is a nonfiction collection of logging stories and other adventures; manly tales, spawned from actual events. A few names have been changed here and there for the usual reasons. Without the encouragement and support of the following wonderful citizens, these tales would be mere memories:

Dave and Mary Busse – Diamond Bar, CA
Bruce Flanders – Speedway Announcer
Tony Fonze – Autorotate Magazine
Peter H. Gillies – Chief Pilot, Western Helicopters
Dave Mittan – 83rd RRSOU – Bangkok, Thailand
Steve Owen – Engineer, Tuba player extraordinaire
Matt Thurber – Aviation International News
Mike and Kathleen Ragenovich - Walla Walla, WA
Jimmy Ray Williams – Gardena, California

To my beloved Lourdes, singing sweetly in Heaven.

Introduction: The T-Factor!

Some kids just got to roll!

It's hard to explain to some people why a person spends most of his life taking chances: Racing motorcycles, flyin' choppers in Vietnam, logging with single-engine helicopters, dangling fireworks in the sky over Disneyland, or marrying pretty Mexican girls. I've been asked that by people who figured I must have a screw loose or maybe I can't read or something. But it's really simple. It's the T-Factor, as in thrills!

Just how a person comes by the disposition that steers them to the fast track, the high wire, or the drag strip is debated by shrinks the world over.

There's no denying it though, if you've got it, you won't be happy unless you get a regular shot of wind-through-hair, burning rubber in high speed turns with lots of G-loads, going flat out on a glassy lake in front a three-thousand horsepower jet-engine, diving off a one-hundred-foot platform (in flames) into a tank of water, or flying through the Golden Arches in a BD-5J, inverted. Not that I've done all that stuff. Well, certainly not inverted! I get motion sickness.

But I know all about the T-Factor, its benefits and its side effects. Lookit: If you've got it, you'll gather no moss. You'll have lots of crazy friends who are good for nothin' beyond having a good time with. You'll meet lots of pretty nurses, and your heart will get all the adrenaline it can drink. I'd call those benefits. The side effects are broken bones, road rashes, high insurance rates, gray-haired parents and wives, paralysis and sudden death.

Nothing ventured, nothing gained, right? I wouldn't have it any other way.

Not that it's dangerous, you see, it's just not for everybody. And those of us who've got it, knew it at a tender age. I was so young that I didn't know the word for what I had, yet. It took a truck driver to educate me, early one Texas morning.

Back 'round about 19 and 49, Mom and Dad ran "Wingo's Trailer Park and Grocery Store," right off of busy Highway 70 going through Plainview. Dad taught school and refinished wood floors while Mom ran the grocery store and kept us four kids under control. If there were any T-Factors in either Blanche or Beauford's DNA, they were recessive, trust me. But they raised a dive-bomber pilot and me, so go figure.

Being the youngest, I was the first to hit the sack every night. I didn't have a history of staying up late, but I was known to swallow coins from the cash register and slip under ladies' dresses who stopped by to have cake and coffee in Mom's kitchen.

So I was just a normal two-point-seven-year old kid, you see? But the strangest thing happened early one morning as I laid there in my bottom bunk bed. I heard my tricycle calling me! My tricycle had to sleep outside, one of Mom's silly rules. It got really lonesome and wanted to go for a ride, and it woke me up! At least, that's the way I remember it.

Was it the rain that made it more fun, I must have been wondering, as my knotty knees sped my excellent tricycle right down those long white stripes some brave person painted long ago, down the middle of Highway 70. I was mesmerized—like a chicken facing a long white line to infinity—and great big trucks were honking and getting out of my way, so I must be doing something right! The smell of burning rubber made it more fun, somehow.

My Mom didn't recall what woke her, but she got up when she heard a faint knocking at the back door. There were a couple of shadowy figures standing outside in the rain under the glare of the bare light bulb. The sign over the unlocked door said "Manager."

Blanche peeked through the Venetian blinds and almost had a heart attack! Jerking the door quickly open, she gasped as she stood five feet away from the Biggest Truck Driver in Texas. A complete stranger, he held her baby son in one big hand and my excellent tricycle in the other. A Really Big Rig idled behind us; its air brakes and rear tires were still smokin'.

As the rain poured off the bill of his baseball cap, the Big Fella asked in the softest male voice she ever heard, "Lady, is this your little boy?"

Us "T-Types" pass it around, you see? The truck driver got his thrill skidding his big rig off Highway 70, and Mom almost got a greasy spot for a kid.

Plainview, Texas—1950

Mark Meets Bildo

Choose carefully the logger you challenge to a fight!

The Gypo-loggers were working the steep terrain twelve miles up the Little Joe River drainage, when "hooker" Mark got acquainted with a sawyer somebody nicknamed "Bildo." Mark hooked up logs on my heli-logging outfit, and he was one of the best on the crew, if you overlooked his in-your-face attitude. He'd never met Bill, who had been cutting logs over on the other side[1] awhile. A stout fellow, Bildo stood six feet tall and was about twice Mark's age.

Mark was a tall man—about six-foot five, I'd say. He was a slender, close-cropped athlete, rumored to have boxed his way through a short tour in the military. But Mark was a logger, no doubt about it. He choked-up some well thought-out, heavy turns. And he ran hard with heavy, nasty coils of wire rope chokers, all the livelong day. He delighted in having back-up turns when everyone else was gasping for air.

Off duty, Mark partied hearty and played basketball like an animal. I stood out of the way and watched when Mark had his hands on the ball and was on a tear. He looked like an albatross when he got wound up and slammed one through the hoop. Mark could one-up just about everyone on the crew.

He had come to us recently from Kalispell, a town that's rough on young lads who are slow to "logger up." A product of the seventies, he grew up a swaggering, street-toughened rebel with the look of a skinhead. "Tool" was his hard-edged rock band of choice, and he didn't take no crap from nobody.

---

[1] Standard logger's alibi for being gone awhile: "I been workin' the other side.... of the mountain."

The morning of the alleged provocation, I flew Mark and Kenny-Bob up to the five thousand foot ridge-top in our outfit's Huey, "Lorena." There was a toe-in "LZ" perpendicular to the ridge, requiring the guys to flow, one-at-a-time, off the skid—and step softly to the ground to keep from jostling Lorena's flaky grip on the log under her aluminum toes.

Mark and Kenny-Bob reached the squat-spot and knelt low. Turning their collars up, both held down their hard hats and daypacks and gave me a thumbs-up. Lorena augured straight up, producing a cloud of dust from her gale-force winds. If my passengers were clean for the ride up, they're dirty now, I mused.

Well above the fir tops, I let her torque turn the tail uphill and then dropped off in a nosedive, woppity-woppin' into the steep canyon. One of those and a cup of coffee are sure to wake you up, first thing in the morning!

Facing south from the LZ, Mark's constant view of Sunshine Mountain kept him in the sunlight most of the long summer workday. The cutters' saws echoed around them as Kenny-Bob finished lacing up his corked boots and took off after Mark, who strode swiftly down the ribboned trail toward the logging strips.

The "saws" were still falling the one hundred-foot-tall, uppermost stand of fir trees above Mark and Kenny-Bob, so the safety word for the day was "heads up!" if you're working downhill! When a cutter starts bucking up a big log lying cross-hill, the various sections can—and frequently do—roll. If that happens, a professional cutter is obliged to yell "Roller!" the same way a courteous golfer yells "Fore!" Unless—of course—he's trying to kill you. In that case, he'll just tee it up and swing from the spikes. Or he'll kick a hesitant two-ton butt log, right on down the hill...

Of course, large rocks, pie-cuts, bears, snooping Woods Bosses, and even helicopters have been known to roll down hill, so heads-up is something one hears a lot on our side of the mountain. Big, round, heavy things can get goin' mighty fast down a steep incline! The ground shakes when a big roller bounces. Rollers continue on their way and splinter large standing trees, knock boulders apart, etc. They are nothing to trifle with!

After dropping off the hookers, I landed the Huey on the dirt road next to the river. Not waiting for my mechanic, I got under the ship and hooked-up the Huey's long-line, testing the electrical/manual releases—top and bottom—in the process. Brushing the dirt off my Carhartts, the radio's external speaker crackled with the usual He-Man banter as the hookers reached their strips and started planning out the first cycle for the morning.

Pretty soon Mark was cussin' a blue streak, something about "one damned too many 'rollers'" comin' his way! What he didn't report over the radio was the string of profanity he shouted at the cutter way up the hill. Little did Mark know, the man he was swearing at carried the only radio among the four saws. Bill seldom had the portable on when he was running his saw. But Mark was new to this crew of cutters – he may not have used much diplomacy right off the bat. And he might not have cared that Bill could "hear 'im talkin' his trash."

Before we knew what was going on, Mark challenged Bildo to a fight. Everyone worked kinda quiet-like after that, but we heard some manly saber-rattlin' over the radio from a certain angry hooker, promising to "teach an old man a lesson." Nary a word from Bildo.

Coincidentally, a new-hire logging pilot had just landed at a nearby airport in our outfit's Cessna, piloted by the Chief Pilot, Dan. They had flown here to give "Dave" his initial logging-pilot check-ride that afternoon, in my Huey....

The cutters always hiked off the hill an hour or so ahead of the hookers, so the hookers took a break in-place while yours truly parked Lorena and drove the company pickup to the airport. I was their Taxi Driver for a preplanned ride to and from the Huey to fly the check-ride amid the final hour of logging.

Once I got Dan and Dave seated in the aircraft and checked out on her little idiosyncrasies, they lit the fire and augured upward—trailing the 175-foot long line—and turned toward the strips.

I jumped back in the truck and cranked up the volume on the logging frequency as I headed up the Little Joe River road, hoping to catch as much of the check-ride as possible. After all, it was "my ship" these guys were logging in.

By the time I drove within radio range of the strips, I detected stress in Dave's voice and heard him say, "Hey fellas, lighten up will ya! I'm on a check-ride here..." It was hot, and Dave had just launched Mark's last turn off the steep hillside and had to abort the overweight log downhill, joining Mark's other turns in a big cloud of dust. I got to the log landing about the time the last three turns came in; Dave was doing a fine job while taking a hammering. I could sense in his tone over the radio that Mark was all pumped up for a fight.

As I blazed down the hill to the Service LZ to whisk Dave and Dan back to their Cessna, I passed by the South Fork campground, where the cutters had a kind of communal camp set up. There were lots of logger's rigs there, already. No one was going to miss the big fight, but us pilots.

Yes, in the forty minutes it took me to drop off the two pilots and say goodbye, I missed the whole fight. But I didn't know that, as I headed back to the South Fork. I saw one of the sawyers coming my way from the campground, and slowed – waving to the driver.

"One-eyed Donnie" had witnessed the whole thing, there was nothing left to see at the cutters' camp. The winner was hosting a victory party at the Traveler's Bar, one of St. Regis' three watering holes. The loser was said to be at a friend's house, coughing up blood from some vicious, down and out boot-kickin.'

"You gonna go congratulate him?" Donnie asked me, figuring that I might be partial to the hooker who just had his clock cleaned. "Sure am," I replied, and spun back toward the bar. [Mark had been warned by Fatty—the Project Manager—that he'd be fired if he couldn't work the next day. But Mark wasn't planning on losing.]

Bildo cut quite the figure, standing there at the bar with a fresh, cold longneck in his big hand, like nothing unusual was going on. He and his cutter pals were buying beers for just about everyone, celebrating his hard-fought thirty-five minute victory. I wasted no time marching up and congratulating him. Amazingly, he didn't look like a man who had been in a fight, except for those peculiar-lookin' puncture wounds on his face. The loggers were drinkin' 'em down and having a good time, so I joined in and eventually asked, "What happened?"

Mark had his corked boots on when his pickup full of hookers drove into the cutters' South Fork camp. He quickly bailed out and made straight for Bill's tiny work trailer. Bill had removed his corks after a hard day's work and had on his old sneakers when he opened his door. "Still want to fight, do you?" Bill asked. Mark was really pumped-up and didn't back off a bit, swearing at the old man for "kickin' rollers down the hill on him," and the fists started flying.

Several sawyers drew close to the action, squaring up with the hookers in a test of their resolve – agreeing on the spot that they wouldn't let the fight spread—and to keep 'em from corking' or killing each other – if it came to that.

It was all Mark for the first twenty minutes. Almost to a man they agreed that Bill was getting his butt kicked, but good. Mark seemed to go crazy, and defying the unwritten logger's code of fair play, Mark knocked Bill down and kicked him in the face with his sharp-tipped spiked boots, drawing blood and causing the cutters to muster up. They stood their ground, though, as Bill kept duckin' and moving. He rolled around and parried several lethal kicks and finally got back on his feet when Mark gasped to catch his breath.

From then on, it was all Bill. Thirty-five minutes into the fight, the cutters moved in and pulled Bill off of poor battered Mark. They had reversed their situations, and many observers were getting worried that Bill would have to be stopped or else. One of Bill's kicks produced a snapping noise that everyone gathered 'round heard clearly. Bill's narrow-toed sneaker sank into an area where most people's ribs attach to their spine, and someone wisely threw in the towel.

Mark was a "no show" for days, and had to be replaced. When he did finally come by the main camp, he wasn't his regular arrogant self – the glint in his eye had faded to a grimace. His after-hours basketball activity was subdued. We witnessed no more after-hour slam-dunks. In fact, Mark had trouble even taking in a good deep breath of air. A tough guy, he downplayed his injuries, but I heard him holler once, just for turning a bit to one side. Mark's kind of butt kickin' would take a long time to recover from, if ever. He'd been on the losing end of this one, and worse—he got beat by an "old man!"

It might have saved Mark a lot of grief if he'd known that "Bildo" was also the winner of his age group at the recent Iron Man competition in Missoula, Montana—when he was working "the other side" of the mountain. It helps to know stuff like that.

The Author near Thorne Bay, Alaska 1993

PARLEZ VOUS LONG-LINE?

Perhaps the Most Fun You Can Have With
a Chopper Strapped to Your Back!

"The fascination of what's difficult
Has dried the sap out of my veins, and rent Spontaneous
joy and natural content Out of my heart."

William Butler Yeats
1865-1939

Thanks, Bill! I couldn't have said it better. And yet the challenge of even describing vertical reference helicopter work has proved to be too much for many of the grown men I work with, my peers, my competition. We be loggin' pilots, we be VertRef Jockeys. We can walk the walk, but talking the talk is another thing.

I recently saw a beautiful documentary film shot during a forest fire, an aerial view of a big tandem rotor helicopter swooping down a ridge. Gliding along far below was a heavy 2,000 gallon water bucket, full to the brim. The mass of quenching water swung magically just over the tops of the pine trees, and at precisely the right moment, "the monkey flipped the switch!" The watery salvo scored an undeniable message to the fire below, and the big helicopter arched up and away for another load from the cold mountain lake. Beethoven's soaring overture Leonore filled the theater.

The video eventually breaks to the flight line. The familiar tandem rotorcraft has just shut down, having saved the day, making it look so easy. The camera zooms in on the pilot who was in the bubble window, a handsome young fellow who just as likely could have been an astronaut. The narrator engages the pilot and soon asks the inevitable: "What's it like to do this kind of work?" And to his credit, the brave young man begins in earnest, trying to put into words what even astronauts cannot. After stumbling over his words for a minute, admits: "I can't describe it!"

Nor should you try, young ace. That's what they pay me to do.

And the only reason I can, sports fans, is because ever since that day, I've thought and thought about the dilemma, and after durned-near nine thousand hours of actual long-line work, I think I have it. You might wanna write this down:

Helicopter long-line work is as close as you can get to fly fishin'...... from the pilot's seat. Whatever you have on the end of your long-line, be it a ponderous water bucket or a 75 pound remote cargo hook – that's the lure. The tree on fire or the man down there in the hardhat, that's the trout. There's just no fly rod to get caught up in the brush.

You, as the pilot (or the monkey, I like to jest) have to be gentle to catch the trout but aggressive to stop the fire. The best VertRef Jockey out there knows instinctively that he must fly the helicopter to a point exactly over the man (or tree) high enough to clear the obstructions (100-to 200-foot trees, usually) and swing his lure into imaginary "sights" which are behind the pilot, below, and under the helicopter.

This positioning must be done with enough speed to be efficient and with enough precision to fine tune the lure as it falls toward the fish, arriving directly over an imaginary plumb line which projects from the helicopter's cargo hook....through the trout.... and straight down to the center of the earth. Do it right, the trout takes the bait. Do it wrong, and critics literally pop out from behind every bush!

If you get in a hurry and flare your gravity-defying machine into position without first attaining stable HOGE power, you fall through. Fishin's over. Fly your line too slowly, the Logging Project Manager will tell you to go park it. (Or on a fire, it will be the Fire Boss!) Knock trees down with your load, you'll be dealing with Smokey. Blink at the moment of truth, and you'll smash your hook into the trout.

You'll lose a friend. And as surely as gravity pulls on everything dear to us, a line of attorneys will be waiting for you at the refueling point, right behind the OSHA guy.

Ignore the pain in your neck and back (and wherever else your seat rubs you for hours on end) and you too will be rewarded with a full creel, or video cameras in your face after every heroic deed. And a pay check for which a chopper driver's girlfriend is compelled to repay him with extraordinary affection.

And how is it that I have come forth on this 19th day of February and finally let go of this well-studied analogy?

Simple: I got up at 05:05 this fine Monday morning, showered and shaved as usual and headed for the kitchen to make breakfast for my working wife and two school kids, only to be met in the hallway by same sleepy-headed wife, asking if I'd forgotten it was President's Day?

No work. No school! Now what? Go back to bed?

"Well, you're a writer, aren't you?" she yawned, while scratching her scalp—then did a one-eighty to the bedroom.

And to this end, Rudyard Kipling once quipped: "The silliest woman can manage a clever man; but it needs a very clever woman to manage a fool!"

"ADIOS, GEARBOX, AND DOWN SHE GOES!"

Another Close Call in Loggin' Country

It was September, 1993. Floyd Hiser and his merry band of flight instructors, mechanics, and various and sundry logging wizards decided (for one reason or another) to leave the flight instruction business behind and go Huey loggin'. Or "Sport Loggin'," as it's known by the yankers and bankers.

And there I was, a freshly trained Huey Loggin' pilot, right off the airliner from Alaska—thinking I was gonna be flying Floyd's "Super 204B!"

As most Huey Loggers will tell you, any good UH-1B and up is fair game for Huey Loggin,' but a "Super B" is 500 pounds lighter, has four more feet of rotor blade and a two foot longer tail boom. Which means *more power*. And Floyd had a "Super B."

But…for reasons unexplained, Floyd let the lease expire on his "Super B" and announced that we would, instead, start out logging with a military surplus UH-1L. I already knew, straight from experienced logging pilot's lips, that the L-Model had a good pull but it swaps ends easily!

The tail boom of the "L" Model is two feet shorter than the "Super B" or the 205 Models, meaning substantially less tail rotor authority. And as I was to learn, trying to dead-lift logs in this ship would lead to my downfall.

I had recently become aware that very few of the outfits logging with Hueys were still using the stock engine-to-transmission drive-shafts, also called "short shafts." Or, for that matter, the old forty-two degree gearboxes. (That's the one which connects to the tail rotor drive shaft and angles it upward to the 90-degree gearbox.) Tougher upgrades of both components were available. But, a zero-time Ka-Flex drive shaft and a Bell 212 forty-two-degree gearbox cost serious money!

So. With the blade figuratively between our teeth, we thrashed our way north from blazing hot southern California toward John Day, Oregon in a leased UH-1L that had never flown log one. The ground pounders followed in our wake with service trailers, spare parts, camping gear, kids, dogs, and one big, heavy, nasty log-grappling hook!

Scott (the chief mechanic) and I took turns flying the ol' bird, while Floyd enjoyed the ride from the aft cabin, strewn with luggage. This bird had the Bell forty four-foot "540" rotor system, which was a plus: rugged and responsive, Cobra style! We took on a load of Jet-A at Carson City, Nevada. Just over two hours later, we squeaked into Burns, Oregon, with 250 pounds left on the dial. The Dash-13 Lycoming slurps 86 gallons per hour, like it or don't. Not far to go. Come sundown, we would be one, with the hornets.

We eventually sailed by, high over our new logging camp, but the Service Landing LZ was still under construction! The last truck load of rock was being dumped to make the Service LZ the only level spot on the mountain. I ended up nosing the Huey into a sloping hillside a couple hundred feet below Service and hovering for around five minutes while Floyd and Scott climbed out and shoved small logs, rocks, and limbs into place under the skids so we could shut down and help with the final preparations.

As the big blades hissed to a halt, untold thousands of obnoxious meat-eating hornets greeted us, an unfortunate plague that the next-highest bidder missed out on. They were thereafter in our faces every moment, except during the hours of darkness.

Early next morning, I fired-up the old Bell, watching in disbelief as the crazed hornets were being blenderized by the main rotor. As their shattered pieces hit the ground, hundreds of the survivors dived on 'em, snowballing and literally rolling around in tennis-ball sized blobs, cannibalizing one another in a bizarre frenzy. Did I mention they have stingers?

I started out with the grapple-hook. This was one of the simplest designs around, but the price was right. At the end of a 175-foot long-line, it was at first a real challenge to manipulate directly over and onto a log, quickly. Once that's done, press the button to close the jaws over the log. Pull like the dickens, pray for translational lift........and away you go! Twenty eight hundred pounds on the scale!

After a few fuel cycles, I got a handle on things. However, I would on occasion pick up a cull log and wouldn't know it until it was in the pile: Big cloud of red dust. Bummer. Keeping my nose to the grindstone, I could eventually build turns by laying logs across one another to fabricate a bonus. There were numerous aborts.

Friends, there are many lessons to be learned by anyone just venturing out in this enterprise, and the first one I learned was: Hot summer Huey Loggin' at 5200 feet pressure altitude on the leeward side of a hogback ridge...for lack of a better expression...sucks!

High density altitudes set in around 10 o'clock on. The leeward winds kicked in thereafter to increase the suction! Throw in a 300 pound grapple from heck, sprinkle generously with a zillion hornets, and the fun goes away.

I began to envy the industry of the less numerous......but larger, bald-faced hornets, who fed upon the smaller meat-eating hornets. Only, their *modus operandi* was to capture their victims on-the-fly; deftly snip off the head, abdomen, and wings; and then roar away with the midsection! Let les miserables clean up the bits and pieces. Hey, I can dig that. I'm a filet mignon-kinda-guy, myself!

My mind drifted back to the task at hand: Maybe we should try it without the grapple. Having "hookers" on the hillside was much less stressful, but each man on the ground would draw around $12 an hour and up. It takes a crew of four or five hookers, two chasers, lots of radios and a hundred or so wire rope chokers to run the average heli-logging show. So. Grapples work out best, at least on paper.

The second lesson I learned was: Never heli-log with a grapple hook that has no hydraulic or electric load-release capability. Our entry-level model used a counterbalance to open the jaws, which meant the pilot had to hang on to his load until it was on the ground before the grapple would release.....which is not a good thing! I pickled the contraption several times to save the ship (and my butt) when a heavy turn would suck me out of the air, big ol' rotors pitching out in the dirty air above me. Low RPM city. Followed by bombs away, hook, line, and sinker.

Well, Floyd always said, "We work to have FUN, and to make money." To illustrate his unerring sense of timing, he took his MD

500D and split for a fine little fire contract in Montana, leaving us with our production problems and our stinking hornets.

Soon after Floyd left, my support group began to fade. Scott cleverly painted several "pickles" on my pilot-side door, and hand-lettered "Pickle King" in close proximity. Pretty funny. If you're an ex-Marine ground-pounder with a nice, safe job. Which I ain't! I was determined to keep trying, regardless.

By the time I had managed to stack up several truckloads of logs on an old skidder path that wound through the woods, it was fairly evident that our production was not cutting it. After the sun rose in the east, 2200 pounds was the most I could dead-lift or otherwise persuade down to the skidder road. We were harvesting around 70,000 pounds per hour, somewhat less than the target of 80,000 pounds per hour the wizards had come up with. I tried being more aggressive, but that only made it scarier.

We eventually resorted to hookers to get the production numbers up. The hookers started out on high-wood, just below the leeward ridge, where a descending easterly flow roiled and boiled. You learn real fast to lead with power early on in the flare to keep from "falling through" when you arrest the swinging remote hook inches above the hooker's head. I was able to pull 40 PSI torque and more until the heat came, but by then we couldn't dial-in enough N1 to keep the turns from drooping. Scott obliged me with the max-allowable engine military-trim adjustment, but, it just wasn't enough. The turns drooped like yesterday's diaper.

Right when I thought things couldn't get any worse, I tried to start up the ship with the main rotor tie-down attached....with three other employees just standing there, watching! My first such no-brainer in over twenty years, and I couldn't believe it. One week into our new enterprise, things began to stink. Then came my replacement.

Well, they didn't call him that, but like the song says, "I was born at night, but it wasn't last night." Scott came up one morning and asked me rather sweetly if I'd mind flying along with this guy to see if he could fly logs (better than me?).

(And, if you don't mind, we'll call this guy "Dick.")

For purposes of insurance, a non-employee pilot (i.e. Dick) wanting to demonstrate his superior logging ability, needed a company pilot to ride along in the right seat during the check-out. Hey! I declined the invitation! I did, however, show "Dick" the usual layout of things, switches, radio setup, etc. And I pointed out the External Load Manual's 3800 pound max hook load limitation, wished him luck, and pulled my helmet out of the plug.

So, since Scott held a commercial rotor-craft certificate, he and Dick went logging! Meanwhile, I jumped on Floyd's Honda 4X4 and roared off into the woods, wanting to see what was being done with "my ship." I listened over the portable radio as Dick relayed everything my detractors wanted to hear, mainly heavier weights! By the time forty-five minutes had gone by, two 4,000 pound turns had allegedly made it into the deck. And watching that bird spin in vertically to the right with the heavy ones made me realize I wasn't near desperate enough to compete with Dick.

Scott appeared to be happy as a clam when he climbed out of the right seat, bragging about how smooth Dick was! "Oh!" I said, "Well, why don't we have Dick show us how to use the grapple while he's here." You could have cut the irony with a machete as I took Dick to one side and, gesticulating with my hands and a stick, gave him a crash course in the use of the accursed grapple.

Off they went again, returning shortly, all warm and fuzzy. I thought for a minute that Dick might hang around to sign autographs, but in short order the entourage of logging wizards and new pilot headed for the nearest cafe (eleven miles!) to savor Dick's angle on things over some fresh baked blackberry pie and hot waitresses......while I gathered my resolve and went back to loggin....now that it was hot again.

And that leads us up to what's happening, Wind Loggers! Within a few minutes, I was back at it, grappling away over the tall, hot, pointy Doug Fir trees. Scott was hunkered in Floyd's trailer, listening over the portable radio as I called out the weights and maneuvered the grapple over a "loner," a stout one-log turn.

It was at this point in time that I became aware of a distinct BANGING coming from somewhere in back, louder and louder, audible even over my custom-made HGU noise-reducing helmet! The sound was a little like King Kong on kettle drums!

I realized I was in trouble and hit the pickle switch, dropping the whole enchilada (again) as I peeled off to the left and downhill. Reducing power and dumping the nose to gather speed, I radioed "I've got a problem!"

Scott was quick to respond, "What's wrong?" To which I replied "I'm not sure, but something's about to let go!" The only chance I had to save the ship was to make it to Service and shoot an autorotation to the only level spot around. I checked the panel: no caution lights! Airspeed 80 knots, Service was one-half mile ahead. I held on to about 250 feet of altitude and called for Scott to "Get behind something, crap may fly."

On a hot final approach, I had to split the difference between two tall pine trees which otherwise blocked the approach to the pad. I knew it would be close, but I only had one shot at it. I sailed right between the tall conifers in a tail-low flare to the pad. As Scott explained later, "Looking out the trailer window, your tail rotor was standing still as you pulled the nose back!"

True enough, when I nailed the collective pitch right over the pad, the ship started turning to the right about the mast: a classic anti-torque failure! Grabbing a handful of throttle, I rolled it off, and the turning stopped 90 degrees right of the final approach heading....and she settled gracefully alongside a big stump at the edge of the pad. Whew. Another squeaker.

I decided to proceed with a turbine cool-down cycle while I cross-checked the instruments for clues....no chip lights! Scott suddenly appeared, opening my left-hand door and extending his hand. He was standing there in as much shock as I. He had already seen the damage and shouted over the racket, "Your forty-two broke!" After shutdown, we could talk without shouting.

"Well, that makes sense," I said, and I began to loosen my grip on the seat cushion and start breathing again. "But no chip light? How could that be?" Going aft with Scott, we checked the forty-two degree gearbox oil level sight-gauge. There was no oil, but there were big chunks of shiny metal where the oil should be. Scott performed an after-the-fact chip-light test, and as I watched from the cockpit, the light came on, nice and bright! Damned protons, who can you trust?

After removing the gearbox, it was plain to see that the internal gears had failed and punched out a big hole in the bottom of the gearbox. I was indeed fortunate to have heard its last gasps in time to accelerate into forward flight, the gearbox thereafter useless all the way to the ground.

At some point, we decided we'd better run into town and let the logging wizards in on our incident, which we did. Still lounging in the cafe, I found Dick and mentioned that I'd flown only fifteen minutes after he left when the problem happened. And, off to one side, I let Scott know that if they hired Dick, they'd also need to hire a relief pilot, 'cause I wasn't going to follow Dick anywhere in rotation.

And no sour grapes, here, I assure you, because before you know it, Dick was on the scene, helmet in hand, and I was a free man. I actually felt relief, knowing I had done my best, and realizing there was no place for me here. Following a long silent drive to the Boise airport, and a quick phone call to Alaska, I was hired on the spot to get my butt back up to Alaska start loggin' in a Bell 214B. Yee-haw!

Within an hour, I was heading north at flight level 340, grinning from ear-to-ear. Hot Damn! The legendary Bell 214B. 2,900 ponies. Blades like barn doors. Glory loggin'. No more L-Model loggin' for me! (Or so it looked. I was still a little naive.)

And it gave me a righteous feeling to realize, as I streaked along into the cold blue stratosphere, that Dick and the wizards were way back there in Hornet City, scratching and clawing for every buck.

I signaled the stewardess: "Another cocktail, please."

Prairie City, Oregon—1993

HELICOPTER LOGGING AND THE IDEAL FIELD MECHANIC

Behind every successful pilot, there is at least one good wrench!

There was something other than the steady snowfall that had me worried that blustery January morning in the winter of '97-98. Montana's logging country was covered with a fresh blanket of Swan Valley's finest powder, but I knew the weather was likely to break around sunrise and I would be flying logs under the Huey all day long. My real concern was this: I had been assigned a new field mechanic. Let me tell you, a pilot with thirty-plus years flying helicopters doesn't take these changes lightly.

Within minutes of introducing ourselves in the blackness of predawn, Alan Martin was literally bleeding all over his aircraft, as well as himself, having sliced the bejesus out of his index finger with a blade honed like a scalpel. The blade came out of his Leatherman tool in an attempt to select a Phillips head to remove the turbine engine's air intake screens. With cold fingers, numb from working in the snow, he did a "Julia Child" on himself. It was a gusher. I heard him gasp as it happened, but he never stopped working.

Alan kept on keepin' on until the job was done, even though I urged him twice to take a first aid break, but he was grinning a grin that I would learn to appreciate in the years ahead. He applied some pressure to the cut and kept marching. As I had just observed, the job comes first with "Big Al."

The helicopter's icy cabin was being defrosted by a 50,000-btu space heater as Al and I continued to wrestle the tarps and blade covers off the cold logging machine, snow having hindered our progress this fine morning. We worked by flashlights and a distant 300-watt halogen flood light which was powered by a humble little Honda generator, purring along somewhere near the tree line. That and the glow of our little service van's headlights were the only comforts we enjoyed on this typical heli-logging Service Landing.

Once all the covers were neatly folded and put away in the van, Alan turned to the first aid kit and began treating his pulsing finger, joking finally about being off to a bad start. We had won the daily race with the sun, as all good heli-loggers do, and now all we had to do was keep that Huey in the air for eight hours or so and my work day would be over…but the mechanic's work day would just be getting started.

Al is 35 years old, lean and strong, and flattering his All-American freckled face rides that ever-present satisfied grin. Beneath that, though, lies an unusual devotion to his ship and his profession. Nowadays it's my Huey, but in the past it was an F-15, an A-10 Warthog, or a little bug smasher.

Air Force trained, this veteran of ten years service was crewing F-15s around the clock in Bahrain when Desert Storm was pounding Hussain's thugs during the Gulf War. He long ago earned a reputation as a sharp, dependable aviation technician, and more than one outfit wanted Alan on their team.

A military brat, Alan was born in Heidelberg, Germany. Following his family around for years, he eventually joined the US Air Force in 1985 with one goal—getting back to Germany! His counselor at boot camp suggested becoming an aviation crew chief, and he soon found himself at Langley AFB, Virginia, taking care of the vaunted F-15 Eagle. He was thereafter transferred to Bitberg AFB, Germany with the proud 53rd TFS NATO Tigers and on to the ZULU Alert Facility.

Alan left Germany in May of '89 and found himself crewing the F-4 Wild Weasel at George AFB, California. While stationed there he met his future wife, Kelly, and son Brad. In September of 1990, Alan was assigned to Desert Shield in Bahrain and crewed F-15s at the then-secret Shakiza Air Base. His Golden Knights kept up an incredible 89% FMC (readiness) rate, earning every crewman in the squadron the Outstanding Unit Award with Valor.

Eventually, the pressures of being away began to affect Alan's family, and he returned to civilian life. This man truly loves the outdoors, especially elk and deer hunting. He was determined to find a niche for his family and himself while employed in the wild expanses of Montana.

It was with Garlick Helicopters in Hamilton that Alan discovered a love affair with an aging fleet of surplus Huey helicopters. These powerful old warbirds, renovated for utility work (such as logging), are simple enough by today's standards for a man with his experience to crew by himself in the field...with a lot of tools.

After a few years of rebuilding the ghost ships of the Vietnam era, Al saw a chance to sign on with a heli-logging company working in Montana, and that, gentle reader, leads us up to our first encounter in the dark near the Canadian border, where Alan bled all over my helicopter.

Since that time, we have worked hundreds of hours together in good weather and bad, and I've never had to worry again about the attention my ship gets after a long day of "wind loggin'."

As fast as the jet fuel tank is filled following the last flight of the day and the big main rotor coasts to a stop, Alan is zipping around opening up the cowlings, undoing the Dzus fastners, and putting his hands on gear boxes and drive shaft bearings to check for tell-tale heat or vibration.

Now, I've had some mechanics who wore fancy rings and regular street clothes on the job, but I've noticed that the best mechanics dress simply, get dirty fast and seldom are clean enough to rub up against. Alan is no exception—he even set off the gas alarm in my motor home once during a brief visit, embarrassing him to no end. Although he was freshly showered and in clean street clothes, the fumes emanating from his tolulene-and oil-soaked shoes were too much for my gas sensor. I thought we'd never get the little siren turned off.

The life of a field mechanic in the Huey heli-logging environment is not for the timid. We keep these machines flying daylight to dark in the winter, and nine-or ten-flight-hour days in the summer are not unusual. That means the wrenches are putting in 15-to 20-hour days at times, always outdoors and normally unassisted.

Add to his maintenance duties the care and feeding of a service truck, service tanker, power generator and numerous Cat-sized batteries, the hourly refueling of the chopper, and a daily maintenance inspection around noon when the pilot shuts the ship down, slowly creeps out to stretch and have a quick snack. This mid-day inspection centers on the critical areas that heli-logging impacts: drive shafts, transmissions, tail boom mounts, engine mounts, cargo hooks, the list seems to go on forever.

These ships have been known to come apart in the air if an undetected crack is left to spread or a hook fails to release a heavy log on command, and I've made a mental note that all the first rate field mechanics put on a race face when they start looking for trouble, armed with a good flashlight and a magnifying glass.

In preparation for this story, I asked Alan what he felt were the key traits of a good field mechanic, and left him alone with a legal pad for awhile. He returned, quick as a bad habit, with a couple of pages of good stuff that I've had to condense for the sake of brevity, but I boiled it down to this:

"Aircraft maintenance is something that is in your blood. It's definitely not for everyone. Being a field mechanic is an acquired taste. This career is not for someone who enjoys the routines of life, but for those who prefer shooting from the hip and who love an adventure!

Favorite quote: 'There's no maintenance short cut worth a pilot's life.'

A field mechanic can actually be home six months out of the year, which is better than a lot of other jobs. The typical logging mechanic schedule is two weeks on, two weeks off. The pay is usually great. The people you work with are quite different than other professions: Loggers! These folks have rough exteriors and unique senses of humor. They surely are a different breed of people. We witness our share of squabbles, even knock-down, drag-out fistfights like in the Gold Rush days where disagreements were settled right then and there! Mostly, we're all just hard workin' mountain men at heart!

One of the more rewarding aspects of this career is working through the night to solve a problem, which enables the work crew to get in a full day's logging…and having the pilot thank you for a "good eye!"

The "good eye" that Alan Martin has developed over the years serves me well, especially during those short fuel breaks we take about every hour. The blades are kept turning during this five-to ten-minute pit-stop, and as the pilot adds up the production numbers or munches on an apple, the mechanic is opening up the panels and looking for cracks, broken longerons, leaks and drips, unusual vibrations or noises.

I've had to do this "walk around" inspection more than once myself to check things out, and I can tell you it takes cojones to inch around a Huey helicopter running at flight idle! The tail rotor is a spinning blur just inches away as you place hands all over the skin of the beast—ear protection required—from all the turbine whine and dual rotor racket; while you dodge the hot stream of jet exhaust flowing from the 1300-horse Lycoming gas turbine engine.

Down one side of the tail boom and up the other, then hopping inside the cabin to check the main transmission gearbox area for signs of stress, leaks; a brief word with the pilot and then out again to spray-lube the remote cargo hook at the bottom end of the long line where the lifting steel meets the log chokers and a lot of wear happens every hour.

After all this, a quick salute from Alan, I roll the throttle back up to 6600 rpm with the confidence I need to return to loggin'!

For an operation that logs an average of 200 hours per month per helicopter, our world would be lost without dedicated aircraft mechanics like Big Al. I am proud to dedicate this story to him and others like him, and those field mechanics of tomorrow that share Alan's zeal for a unique and rewarding career out there in "God's Country."

LOGS THAT PUNISH!

External Load Hazards Learned the Hard Way

There was a lot on my mind when I signed up to be a single-engine helicopter-logging pilot, starting with a long list of debtors and ending with three dead pilots. The debtors were being taken care of—it was simply matter of living long enough to pay them all off. Something that Bill, Joe, and Hugh would worry about no more.

The demise of three logging pilots had created job openings in their passing, and although grateful for an opportunity to learn the trade, I would also be flying in the general area of the accidents, and working beside and over friends and co-workers of the deceased. Over time, they made sure that I didn't lose focus on the hazards that come from snagging heavy loads and yarding them into thin air…and back down again, over there.

Joe was thought to have been at the controls when the Bell 214B noisily yarded in a hooter — just south of Dora Bay, Alaska. One of the hands on the log deck at the time told me he thought the log weighed around seven thousand pounds: max end-of-cycle weight. The log hung vertically from a beefy, thirty-five foot wire-rope choker, hooked at the end of a 175-foot long line. Joe brought it in smoothly, as veteran production logging pilot Bill jotted down the numbers from the right seat. Bill was the Chief Logging Pilot and one of the most experienced 214 logging pilots on the planet at the time.

This particular turn—most likely seven hundred board feet of valuable Sitka Blue Spruce— settled vertically onto the apron of the log deck—observed by the chasers and loader operators. That's apron, meaning it may have settled prematurely—on top of another log lying near the log deck.

The view from two hundred feet might not have alarmed the pilot: His load had stopped, yet the helicopter continued to descend for an instant—just enough to create slack in the long line. As Joe added power to keep the choker taut, the vertical log allegedly slipped off the horizontal log and fell probably no more than a foot— abruptly – with the burly helicopter now pulling in the opposite direction. In doing so, the unloaded helicopter was hammered by the full weight of the log just inches off the ground, resulting in a very rude pop!

According to one witness, there was no radio feedback from the ship. The 214's emergency siren never came on, but it was all too clear that the 2900-horse "Heavy Lifter" was coming down in a left turn. Her rotors were alleged to be turning at the normal RPM, the "dash 55" turbine engine was singing right along—but from all the noise and erratic wobbling, the ship was clearly in trouble.

The 214 impacted the ground next to the log landing—in the same left bank—with little or no deceleration, and was destroyed on impact. The ground crew was on the scene quickly, in time to comfort the dying pilots as an air ambulance was summoned from the Alaskan Coast Guard.

In the long, slow process of litigating everything through to closure, the cause of the accident was alleged to have been the fracture of one of the three major hydraulic servos that command the tilt of the 214's swash plate. One of the cyclic servo upper control rods allegedly broke just below the swash plate, making control of the logging machine impossible at that point.

The fracture appears to have initiated as a hairline crack that allegedly went undetected. The abrupt hammering by the heavy log finished off the link and brought the aircraft down. A tragic affair, to be sure.

Heli-loggers refer to this type of hazard as a hangman's turn, after the abrupt jerk designed into the old Wild West gallows. Those unfortunates receiving capital punishment plunged boots-first through a trap door, allowing them to free-fall to the terminus of a slack hangman's noose—guaranteeing there'd be no controversial "survivors." (Heavier prisoners were sometimes decapitated in the grim application of justice, and well-dressed folks began to avoid the front row seats.)

Hugh—bless his heart – was informed by the hooker working in heavy timber under his Bell Super 204B that "smoke was coming out of the tail rotor." The Service Landing was almost two minutes away. Instead of pickling the line and landing miles away from his mechanic, he chose to fly to Service.

He made it that far, and began setting the long-line down neatly. The bearing that had been smoking up to that point suddenly froze; the tail rotor and ninety-degree gearbox departed the aircraft, and Hugh didn't survive the crash, which also injured his mechanic.

Hanging logs also occur in multiple log turns, as "Captain Tom" could tell you. In the process of hoisting up several logs that fly out as one turn, the hooker is often the only one that can see this situation developing. The pilot may already have the turn in the air before anyone notices the heaviest log riding in the gnarly branches of the other logs.

At the time, Captain Tom and I were logging with two Hueys in the same valley back near Panther Creek, Idaho. We operated off a common FM radio frequency and flew the logs to the same landing—which was a lot of fun, by the way.

Things were going along quite merrily that morning; maybe we should have known something was up! Tom reared back on a big four-log turn of fire-salvaged timber hooked up by "Booboo," a handsome muscle-bound hooker, and friend to all. I heard Booboo's manly voice radio "Clear," which was Tom's signal to let-er-rip!

A half-mile to the west, I was lowering my remote hook to a hooker named "Scooter," who just about had his leather glove on the remote hook. Suddenly we heard Booboo's radio call—a shook-up, almost girly-voice said, "Tom is goin' down!!"

I halted my descent with a handful of pitch and pulled the hook up and away from Scooter, peeling off to the east and climbing. Tom's UH-1H came into view as I topped the bald, rolling hill between us.

His ship was still in the air, but just barely. With her main rotor-blades pitched up and coning, the helicopter was floundering just twenty feet above the sloping terrain. Large clouds of black dust billowed here, there, and up the hill attesting to the hard impact of several logs and the long line that he had just pickled.

Tom had managed to return to controlled flight at a very low altitude! Finally able to speak, Tom verbalized his displeasure in terms

I am not at liberty to repeat then managed to blather back to Service, where he landed gently, shut down—and took a nice, long break.

His A&P mechanic (Dennis "the Menace") methodically combed over the helicopter, looking for hammered lift-links, twisted drive shafts, busted engine mounts, [stains in the seat cushion], wrinkles in places where there should be none, and so on.

Captain Tom had been caught totally flatfooted by the powerful jolt that the dead-falling log had given him, perhaps a second or two after launching the turn off the steep hillside. Booboo had been taken by surprise as well, observing the heavy black log slide rapidly out of its brothers' burnt limbs – too late to holler "slack choker!" over the radio.

Tom was wearing the standard lap belt, yet was knocked halfway out of his seat. In this mode, he lost control, time, and altitude scrambling back to his rightful place behind the cyclic and getting his feet on the pedals. Had to be scary. (Knock on wood.)

Tom's mechanic found no obvious damage after a long look, and the brave little pilot went back to work, much the wiser and twice as cautious. (And his lap-belt a bit tighter.)

On the "Tipton" burn salvage sale near
Prairie, Idaho—December '93.

That...was No Mechanic!

Differences are settled abruptly in Loggin' Country.

One of the finest loggin' pilots I ever had the chance to fly beside was a guy we'll call "Chuck," if you don't mind. Chuck and I first met up near White Pass, Washington a decade ago. I was a rookie Captain, logging in my favorite helicopter of all time, the awesome Bell 214B. You know the one: Rotor blades like barn doors; 2900 rabid ponies; 7,000-pound lift capacity. And a reputation as a widow-maker, Chuck would tell you.

Chuck was a "re-hired" pilot. He came back from wherever he'd been, toting a ton of loggin' time. The Powers That Be needed to keep Chuck busy for a few days, and I needed a good stick. He wound up on my shift early one morning, a big fellow with a neatly trimmed beard and a conservative smile. I introduced myself—shook that big right hand of his—scooted over to the right seat, and off we thundered.

On the way down into the canyon toward the steep sale, I briefed Chuck about the bird's little idiosyncrasies, including the hair-trigger remote-hook switch. And sure enough, he pickled a "five- drop" of wire-rope chokers his first choker call. I tried not to do a double-back flip, but I was waxing toward skeptical.

"Oops," he said deeply, a few seconds later. He had merely brushed the tiny (Radio Shack) remote switch with his little finger and five coiled chokers sailed for the tall hemlock stand below us. (We were already short of chokers, of course.) "Why would Radio Shack put such a tiny little switch on such a big bad helicopter?" I asked Chuck, tongue in cheek. "Real switch on order?" he inquired, politely.

Chuck was rumored to be a Real Loggin' Pilot. Turns out, he had an A&P license, too. As far as I was concerned, he earned major points

39

for technique on the first tricky turn we pulled. "Ten o'clock and three hundred," hooker Kit called in his position over his pack-set.

With minimal searching, Chuck spotted Kit in the shadows near a brushy swale—waving a bright orange ribbon streamer in the dawn's early light.

"Got 'cha," Chuck responded.

Chuck dumped collective pitch – (just right—no over-speed), slid in some right pedal and reefed back on the cyclic—flaring a little to the right. I watched out my bubble door as the distant remote hook began a gorgeous decelerating-looping maneuver. Kit stood frozen as the hook zeroed in on him, then he continued…

"I got a Skip-and-Vern-turn for you, Cap'n." When the empty remote hook cleared the last tree and hovered at arm length, Kit keyed his mike, "Where the hell's my five-drop?!"

"I'll get back to you on the sissy-drop; let's rock." Chuck quipped. Kit scrambled away as Chuck pulled the slack out of the chokers and started his big windup.

Reefin' to get the two logs aligned and rarin' back as far as the 200-foot long non-twist wire cable would allow, he craned his neck hard left in the bubble window and stuck the fragile, snarling tail rotor comfortably between two nearby Doug fir tops. The hooker finally hollered, "Let 'er rip, tater-chip!" and we were off like that proverbial prom dress!

Followed shortly thereafter by a short "five-pound" cedar log—and a long skinny red fir, launched smoothly into the cool morning air toward spectacular, snow-covered Mount Rainier. The old volcano sported a leaning stack of pearl-colored lenticulars on the Yakima side.

"Six point zero on the weight," Chuck read off the load cell. There was none of the roughness and tranny-static-stop-bangin' goin' on that I had feared. Yours truly can live without any of that!

Everything in the green, AFCS blips all lined-up, no strain on the tail boom. I wrote down the data on my knee-board Logging Report. A minute or so later, we might as well have been in the movies as Chuck made a speedy but accurate drop-off of "Skip and Vern" at the log landing, with minimum back lash from the big cedar, and no fracturing of the long, slender log.

"Chokers!" called the chaser boss.

One of the toughest maneuvers in logging is getting a heavy turn down quickly—then picking up a load of chokers (100 feet away) with no wasted motion. The secret is handling the power-down and torque extremes by anticipating the precise touch needed—smoothly. How hard could it be?

I observed the action as Captain Chuck deftly pulled the slack out of his choked-up turn, hovered sideways a couple of feet toward the chasers—maintaining just the right amount of strain on the line. Triggering the remote release switch, Chuck added just a frog's hair more right cyclic. This amounted to mere body English, a subtle dip to the right, then left cyclic: a subtle rocking motion.

The remote hook appeared to have eyes. The chaser boss nonchalantly slapped Kit's five-drop on the gnarly load beam, hovering at arm's length. Tiny pedal movements made all the difference. Smoothly done!

"Nice hook," drawled the chaser, who resembled a pirate in his corked boots and tattered tin pants. "Nicely done," I complimented the driver.

[Or, "You're as good as your last time at bat," in this business.]

Heck, I'm thinking: We could do this all day and live to cash those impressive paychecks! I took a gander at the panel: In the green, no segment lamps illuminated; 130 gallons of dinosaur juice in the bag. Pour the coals to 'er! I began to relax and enjoy the fantastic view, our big fat rotor blades banging out tunes from Rotor Heaven.

Another big turn is waiting, a "root-wad" Kit has choked up near the top of the tree-length blow-down. Chuck nimbly spotted the five-drop on the orange ribbon blob and bee-lined the heavy remote hook over to Kit. Slapping the lone choker eye into the remote, Kit hollered, "Rip and tear!" and took off through the thick, wet brush.

Waiting a second for Kit to clear, Chuck reefed the three-ton root-wad up and over, using mondo leverage to break the holding roots. Laying it down in line with the pull, we heard a loud snap far below us, above all the noise from the barn doors and three thousand flaming mustangs. The tree-length turn shuddered, then dropped to the ground in full submission as Chuck kept the thirty-foot choker taut—avoiding a rude jolt.

"It broke," Chuck observed. One more skillful flop back over to the starting position—another stimulating launch—and six hundred board feet of Douglas fir was learning to fly. Couldn't have done better, myself!

"Six point six, nice stick." Chuck had 'em eating out of his hand now.

"Dan-a-beau! You're gonna love this!" Kit radioed to one of his logging mates.

By the end of the day, everyone was "spanked," which is what we came for. There were over ten truckloads of logs on the ground, the lenticulars around the old volcano were on fire, and the landing crew was swamped.

You might be surprised to learn, what I admired most about Chuck wasn't his flying, it was his post-flight inspection. Turns out, he was a mechanic from way back. But Chuck learned his mechanic's stripes the hard way—as an apprentice, not at a school, or in the military.

He had done his share of pumpin' Jet-A1 and getting' greasy. Chuck repaired his own rollin' stock and took an active interest in all things mechanical around his helicopters. Some loggin' pilots I've worked with walk straight to their rig after a long day of loggin'—not Chuck.

It would seem that he had taken the cowlings off a hot 214B so often that he could do it blind-folded. I stood out of his way but looked over his shoulder as he pointed to the high-tech rubberized Nodamatic parts that were wearing out here and there.

"This grommet is technically within limits, but we better get another one on order," he announced to Jack, the ship's lead mechanic. Then on to the next layer, the "speeder box," the tricky "J" channel. On to the tail boom, noting metallic mung in places that were wearing, if you knew where to look. Then he put it all back together, updated the required log books and finally hit the twelve-mile-long, muddy jeep trail back to the motel by the twilight's last gleaming.

This gets us through the part of the story where everything is hunky-dory and all hands are happy. I lead you now to a place of reckoning, where I hope to shed light on an ingredient essential to things being hunky-dory in the first place: Professionalism! Which is what Chuck's logging mechanic apparently forgot about, a few years down the road.

We shall know him only as "Dick." Chuck and Dick had worked on and off together at a remote, large-scale logging operation for over a year. The logging machinery of choice was the K-Max helicopter—a fairly new machine.

This pilot/mechanic relationship was not a marriage made in heaven. Dick was alleged to be one of those mechanics who didn't like pilots in general, and Chuck in particular. And Chuck figured he'd forgotten more about wrenching on flyin' machines than Dick ever knew. And it musta showed.

So one day, Dick's nap in the maintenance trailer was rudely interrupted by that windy K-Max of Chuck's, which had just landed for the (short) noon maintenance break. Chuck poked his sweaty head into the shady shed and complained to Dick about the remote hook being dry—needing some grease. Dick got up from his folding chair and huffed off to get the grease gun.

After a quick lunch in his rig, the good Captain climbed back into his workhorse and returned to the blue sky. Soon he heard from every hooker on the job that the @#*!+ remote hook was puking grease everywhere! Chokers were slipping and shooting off the load beam – a dangerous mess!

Back to the service landing he flew. Getting out for a look, it was apparent to Chuck that a freshly packed grease gun had been emptied into the remote hook, when two small squirts would have been plenty.

Storming into the maintenance trailer, Dick sensed the Captain's anger, but Chuck's right jab still caught him by surprise—flush on the nose—and he stumbled out of the trailer (in front of a factory rep, no less)—twisted his knee, and crashed onto the hard, humbling dirt.

Word of such attitude adjustments gets around in Loggin' Country, "Where men are men and sheep can hear a zipper a mile away." And I never figured ol' Chuck to resort to his fists…but the more I thought about it, the more interested I was in hearing his version over a cold Dr. Pecker or two.

Jump forward to January of Ought Two: Chuck leaves a note on my motor home in Saint Regis, Montana—something to the effect that he's loggin' in nearby Superior. Said he might catch me later. Meanwhile, I was Huey loggin' out by Tamarack Creek, not far away.

Sure enough, a day or so later I was taking my mid-day maintenance break when Chuck drove up in his shiny pickup. Grinning broadly, I shook that famous right hand again, and invited Chuck to join me on the tailgate.

We tried in vain to catch up on all the years gone by, but I had to get back to work. Before you know it, we said "adios" and I was back slinging larch and pine logs through the air.

Several minutes later—figuring that Chuck had already left the service landing—I radioed my mechanic, Big Al. "Hey Al, got a copy?"

"Right here Dorc, go ahead," Big Al replied.

"Chuck's claim to fame is—he punched out his mechanic!"

To which Big Al replied, "Well, he's standing *right here,* I'll put him *on....*"

I immediately felt embarrassed for saying anything about it over the radio. Then that deep, friendly voice came back over the frequency: *"That....*was no *mechanic!"*

Left seat in the mighty 214B:
Clint Burke hoists a *bonus-tronus-tag* near Pendleton, Oregon-1995

WHEN ROTORS DEPART...

It Breaks More Than Your Heart.

Come with me, fearless reader, to the place where widows dwell. That dark and uncomfortable place where old stick buddies wipe the beer off their gray mustaches with a dry sleeve and recall the good old days, before the time that Captain Bill's rotor system took off all by itself, leaving him and his UH-1B fuselage holding on to a heavy load of logs.

Despite the hard-won ATP rating in his flight suit's right leg-pocket, his aristocratic good looks and a gorgeous young bride waiting for his return, he was no longer hovering 200 feet over beautiful Washington. And despite the powerful Lycoming turbine engine's contribution—the Huey's rapidly spinning mast, swash plate and tail rotor—gravity was in control.

Consider the mind-blowing experience as Captain Bill's mechanic listened over his portable radio: They were having a friendly chat about something irrelevant to the current situation while Bill logged away, nearby. Captain Bill was in mid-sentence when his mast separated at the damper splines and his coveted metal rotor blades headed skyward, uninhibited.

The mechanic and the woods crew all heard the last words from "Flash Sikorsky" in that terrible instant, and the echoing crash. Bill had no warning. It was a hell of a way to check out. A sad day for us Huey loggers, let me assure you.

Bill would rest better on high, knowing the cause was quickly found and that his widow would be taken care of—following a long, glacier-like legal process. He would also rest easier knowing his demise got the attention of those of us who fly logs for a living in the old war birds.

He might not understand why Captain Tom was in such a hurry to join him up yonder, hardly a year later.

Alberton, Montana, has been home to loggers forever, it seems. Why, there's a familiar little sign in just about every store window around them parts that boasts, "WE SUPPORT THE TIMBER INDUSTRY!"

Log trucks, diesel-powered log loaders, logging scales, beat-up old crew-crummies, chainsaw shops, old-style misery whips—you see all kinds of logging stuff in Alberton. Our heli-logging crew drove thru the little town at o-dark-thirty every morning on the way to the high snowy country along Petty Creek Road.

Back then we had a big feller flying relief for us; Captain Tom had flying credentials on top of flying credentials. He could fly whatever it was, and the box it came in—if you were to make inquiry. And he was no stranger to single-engine heli-logging. According to some of the guys on the ground, he also had an attitude. And that may help explain where his head was on that cold November Montana morning, as he flew away with one of "Rosey's" turns.

"Hey, Captain Tom! Your ship sounded kinda funny when you took off with them logs," Rosey advised. (Us Huey pilots get that all the time, it's usually the bleed-air heater. It makes a shrill cycling sound when it's crankin' out the BTUs.)

"Ummph. Sounds okay to me," came the Captain's gruff reply. On toward the log landing he lumbered. Then back to the next hooker for another turn.

"Yeah, Captain, I heard it too," radioed Stinky Bob, "a bad, swirlin' noise." 'Bout now, the boys are getting' fearful. They weren't born yesterday, and they don't need no Huey lying upside down in their strips, slowing things down.

"I don't hear nothin', ship's flyin' fine," responded Captain Tom. Another big load of logs hits the log landing.

As yet another four-thousand-pound, snow-covered red-spruce-and-Douglas fir load heads for the landing, the knot bumper named Rosco looks up from his chain saw toward the oncoming menace. The swirling blades are making a gosh-awful sound, the likes of which he's never heard in ten years of heli-logging. He drops his saw, runs to his truck and comes back with a radio in his hand.

"Git that sombitch away from me, pilot. There's somethin' bad wrong with that chopper."

Finally, language that the good Captain could understand. He punched the load off into a pristine patch of some would-be Christmas trees and headed for the Service Landing, listening intently now for the sound that merited the concern of his thoughtful crew. His heartbeat cranked up a notch or two.

The Service Landing was a scant quarter mile away. Captain Tom could see the old Freight Liner belch black smoke as the mechanic hit the starter. Marvin was anticipating a routine refuel-and-turn-around. Not listening to his radio, most likely.

Halfway to Service, a two-foot chunk of one main rotor blade—out near the trim tab—has had enough of this round-and-round-she-goes business, and departs with prejudice and great fanfare.

Imagine the reaction of a distant deer hunter: He's been hiding in the thickets, knowing them stupid deer can't hear him approaching over all the logging noise. The helicopter's blades 'been sounding kinda different lately, but heck—he's just a deer hunter. What does he know about rotor blades?

Suddenly the chopper sounds like death on a stick, like nothing he's ever heard before! And through the clear blue sky streaks a terrible noise, sounding something like "I'm comin' to kiiiiiill you, deer hunter."

Before he can lock and load, the racket dissipates to a wounded Frisbee sound and a big chunk of honeycomb aluminum crashes into a nearby Tamarack. It topples harmlessly through the limbs overhead and falls at his feet. He now knows what the chopper's blades are made of, and learning more all the while.

We should really get back to Captain Tom. He's still up there in that thing, doing a dance known only to those who have tried to spin-dry a heavy wet rug all by itself. (In the words of a Tombigbee River pilot I once read about, "The music was playin' faster than he could dance to.")

The Captain rightly figgers he's about to die, and like Bill, he wasn't quite ready. There was nothing on the panel he could make out—it was one big, goofy blur, as he was being swirled rudely around in the cockpit—trying hard to visualize a clear place to put 'er down!

And I seriously doubt that anyone could have done a better job, neither, cause Captain Tom managed to part the sea of trees below him and got the toes of the skids on some steeply sloping ground. There was some incidental damage as he lowered the pitch and the tail feathers buzzed through some short re-prod. The old bird abruptly came to rest, right off the shoulder of the road to Service. Whew! Cancel the tombstone.

Unlike another recently departed Husky pilot, Captain Tom's blade lost a big chunk but he made it to the ground in one piece. Captain Tom posed for a photograph with obvious relief—toasting with a cold, freshly opened sixteen-ounce can of beer. Nobody would fault him for celebrating his new lease on life. Not Captain Bill, and certainly not me.

A Boot Full of Trouble!

A Close Call in Logging Country

It was first light, March 23rd as I steered the '63 vintage Bell UH-1 "Huey" to 5,000' MSL through a light Montana snowfall. On board was a crew of four heli-loggers who needed to be put out on a sharp ridge west of St. Regis. Once on the ground, they would start hiking toward their strips and choking up the freshly fallen logs. Snow was part of the adventure; nothing new to us loggers. I was dressed for the occasion and ready for whatever, or so I thought.

We hadn't had to fly our hookers up since the rotor blade change a week prior, so this was our first trip into the new LZ. This particular hog-back wouldn't accommodate a full-down skid landing, so I had to hold a low hover while the team members unbuckled and methodically moved toward the door to step down onto the skid, then step to the ground.

This we've done as a team many times before, but something went wrong as Ted, the hooker team leader, stepped on to the left skid. Slowly we began to drift left into some jagged brush, even though I was giving the cyclic hard right and aft inputs. The drift speed relentlessly increased as Jeff, the next man in the door, began to step down.

By this time I knew we were in trouble and Ted could see it on my face through the bubble window. Coming up ahead was a towering yellow pine that had been left standing inside the thin-cut. It had our number written all over it!

The terrain was too steep to consider rolling off the throttle, and doing so would have put my good buddy Ted, and the rest of us, in a serious hurt. Realizing I had still had one dimension left to work with,

I reefed up the collective pitch to red line torque and held on as we accelerated toward the big pine, those big Huey rotor blades shattering the air as we shot up and just over the treetop, the top-most pine needles sailing by under Ted's boots—a picture now permanently etched in my memory—while Ted scrambled back onboard, Jeff's strong hands helping to pull Ted in by the neck. I could hear Ted's stressed voice over the din, "What the.....!"

The ship quickly stabilized climbing out with airspeed and with everyone back in their seats. We returned to controlled flight and started to breathe again. I radioed to the rest of the crew that we had had to abort our crew insertion for mechanical reasons and were heading back to the Service LZ.

Following an uneventful four-minute cruise down the steep Little Joe Creek drainage to our Service LZ, Marvin, our trusty A&P mechanic, was anxiously awaiting our safe arrival, portable radio in hand.

After about ten minutes, Marvin found the cause of our near disaster: a metal Cannon plug had been installed by an airport-based avionics shop the previous week (during the time that I was on break).

Somehow the Cannon plug was part of a left-cyclic mic-switch replacement job, which the avionics shop technician allegedly performed while our rookie mechanic was on top of the ship tending to a main-rotor-blade-replacement/tracking mission.

The part of the avionics job that apparently didn't get finished was the all important task of securing the Cannon plug to the (provided) threaded stud, with an Adel clamp. Worse yet, the Cannon plug was apparently laid loose in the area just aft of the cyclic control, and in the small space that the cyclic gimbal must move to have full cyclic travel in all quadrants.

The cyclic-base leather dust boot was then bolted back into place using six hex bolts, guaranteeing no one else would see the ticking time bomb. It took over forty hours of flying before the Cannon plug finally worked into the critical area and prevented normal cyclic travel to the right and aft. This couldn't have come at a worse time: letting passengers out while hovering in a tight LZ!

Due to the seriousness of the SNAFU, I took it upon myself to call the NTSB Field Office in Seattle, as required by AIM, Section 6, which deals with reporting malfunctions of flight controls, among others. I hesitated almost a week to involve the Feds in this near disaster, but in the interest of safety, I felt I had no choice.

When common sense is called for, anything less can be scary. When aviation professionals stop thinking, people can and do get hurt. We were lucky survivors, and our story needed to be told. As of this writing, I understand the technician involved no longer works there.

Meanwhile, I am thinking how good it is to see the sun rise each day, the ship in one piece....Ted and Jeff running around in the timber below me, chokin' up turns, laughing over the radios.

Ted's wedding day is coming up soon and we plan to be around to help him get hitched. And we pause often to remind ourselves that we were *that close* to meeting our Maker just a few days ago!

Big Al's "Heads-Up" Award!

"Power tools, power tools!" cried Chicken Little!

The highlight of my helicopter-logging day came when I finally got to set that last turn of stupid logs down in the Log Landing and head for Service. Eight hours in the saddle was plenty for a guy who's long in tooth. My bod would literally tingle when I could finally sit up straight in the seat—stretch out on those beefy "Bell Huey" tail rotor pedals, and fly straight and level for a minute or so. Take me now, Jesus—while it feels so damned good!

Second to that would be the noon "maintenance break." Beside lunch, I mean. It's sooo satisfying to peel one's sore butt out of the saddle after hammering it for five hours plus and let "Big Al" ("Mr. Good Wrench") check over "Lorena" while yours truly ("Captain Methane") limps like a cripple—over the crusty snow—to the toasty service truck. Al usually had it all warmed up for me.

Once seated, I'd scan the weak radio waves for a distant, scratchy Paul Harvey or some News From the BBC. I listened to the world fall apart while consuming the contents of my lunch bucket: Chicken wing; BBQ-beans; Cole slaw; and Yoplait. (Who put this Beano tablet in here?) Wash it all down with a cold Dr. Pecker for a jolt of caffeine, and Captain Methane is ready for the last two cycles.

Big Al usually took thirty minutes or so to perform an honest inspection of the UH-1H for hot bearings, cracks, leaks, chafing lines—things that'll git 'ya in this line of work. (Except for burning up the old jet-tanker, Al had a perfect safety record so far.)

The noon maintenance break became such a cool routine that Big Al and I got real comfortable with each other's work habits over the years. One thing he always did for me on cold days was preheat the Huey's cabin—with a kerosene space heater—five minutes or so before crank time. I never could stand climbing into an ice-cold helicopter and cramming on a frigid flight helmet, say nothing of all the foggy windows and bubbles I needed to see through. Al respected that and saw to it that I started out cozy.

And then it happened! We were logging just west of Tamarack Creek—near St. Regis, Montana. It was a quarter to one on a cold, but sunny December afternoon. Al signaled that he was all done with his maintenance check and headed into the maintenance trailer, toting his heavy canvas bag of tools. I moseyed back to the ship, happy to be getting the last three hours of logging started, after I did my customary walk-around-the-ship preflight.

As soon as I began my walk-around, I sensed that something was already wrong. I couldn't put my finger on it, so I further scanned the area with my Okie sensors on acute, while securing my lunch bucket behind the left pilot's seat with a bungee cord. Then I realized what the problem was: It was too danged quiet, and too danged cold!

The noisy space heater was sitting in the rear cabin area, all right—but Al had spaced plugging in the power cord. I hollered loud enough for Al to hear me, "Thanks a lot, Pee-Pee!!"

(Al's big brother, Terry, gave him his other nickname, long ago—one that Al didn't particularly care for.) After plugging the heater in, I slid the cabin door shut and keyed up the Motorola portable radio—checking with Terry (yes, Al's big brother) to see if the boys were ready to start logging.

"Waitin'on you, Dorc," came Terry's Texan-tinged sarcastic reply.

By that time, Big Al was on hand, scrambling around – apologizing, flustered that he had forgotten to preheat the cabin. I climbed into the chilly left seat, making light of Al's omission, and had the big rotors turning in no time. Blasting thru my mental checklist, the windscreens were just beginning to un-fog when I throttled 'er up to 100% N2. Al waited patiently for my nod, then removed the rosy-red space heater and reclosed the cabin door.

Returning Pee-Pee's crisp salute, I leaned hard left into the bubble and rolled over onto my achy left hip, into the familiar position. With a little spurring, up sprang good ol' Lorena, like a rested workhorse.

I urged her over and up with the 185-foot Kevlar long-line, picking it cleanly off the snowdrifts, weaving around the brushy clumps until the heavy remote hook arose from the orange-painted mud at Al's feet. A right pedal turn put me on track, and I headed up the hill toward the logging strips, a mile or so distant.

"Lorena's headed your way, Tex," I radioed the Landing.

"'Need you to take a saw to 'Johnny-wad' before you haul any logs," Terry informed me, so I bee lined in the knot-bumper's direction. A minute later, I decelerated from eighty knots and brought the remote hook in smoothly to the knot-bumper's chute, where "Pie-Cut" was supposed to be standing with a chain-saw-on-a-rope.

"So where is Pie-Cut?" I had to ask. Looking down from my high hover, I could see Terry and two chasers jogging to hook up the saw. Oh, there's Pie-Cut, yonder! Temporarily indisposed behind a nearby Royal Fir. (You see everything from up here!)

Holding my lofty hover, I watched Terry jog under the left skid. Suddenly, out of the corner of my eye, I saw something streak to the ground, smacking into the mud a few feet ahead of him. The impact made a big muddy splat, causing Terry to reel backwards and stare up at the hovering Huey. The sky is falling?

"Something just fell off your chopper!" Tex exclaimed into his chest-pack radio. My Okie brain raced to think of something vital in the inventory of whirling parts surrounding me that might have just fallen off of some other indispensable part, but Lorena was hovering happily—the gauges were in the green – and I began to wonder. Big Al suddenly chimed in on the Service radio, "Did I hear that something fell off the helicopter?!" "A-ffir-ma-tive, Pee-Pee," I replied, knowing he'd be interested.

"What is it, Tex?" I inquired of Terry. [Mud and ice chunks do fall off the skids from time to time, but that looked like neither nor]. Terry glanced back up at the Huey and cautiously proceeded underneath toward the item(s). He stooped down and gathered the muddy pieces into his big, freckled hands.

"It broke into three chunks," he drawled. "One piece is a fourteen-volt-DC battery pack that says "Milwaukee" on it!" (Not "Bell," I was happy to hear.)

A power tool? A heavy, crack-your-skull-open, two-hundred-dollar power-tool? Pee-Pee always set his power driver down on the left engine deck before he climbed down from the ship. Once his hands were free, he'd stuff the driver into his canvas tool bag—and plug in the heater with monotonous regularity!

(Amazing that the tool stayed on the shroud-less engine deck for the long, breezy flight up the hill—smooth pilot?)

Getting back to Pee-Pee, you probably could have heard him without a radio at that point, for as soon as he heard his brother say "Milwaukee," he let out one of those sky-cracking Charlie Brown *Arrrgghhhs* that came from way deep down in his pocketbook, trailing off at long last into a death rattle. Poor Pee-Pee!

Captain Methane was, of course, equally at fault for not catching it. I allowed a cold cockpit to distract me from finishing my walk-around, where I definitely would have seen the power tool sitting on the engine deck at eye level. But I didn't. And that's the argument I used to console my mechanic when the day was over and the pieces of his power tool were returned to Service in a (used) brown paper bag.

"It takes two sets of eyes, amigo, and I let us down," I told Al. "We're awfully lucky that no one got hurt. Your drill can be replaced, your brother can't," and so on....

"It wasn't mine," he whimpered, waiting for me to shut up. "It was Larry's!" Pee-Pee cradled his fastidious relief-mechanic's shattered drill armature in his grimy, freckled fingers. "I borrowed his Milwaukee 'cause my POS quit workin'. There goes Christmas," he lamented.

Always one to have a cartoon suited to the occasion, I quickly whipped out a sketch that carried the headline, "Big Al's Heads-up Award!" Under the title was a caricature profile of Tex with his big red beard and hardhat, looking up – but with a Milwaukee power-drill half-imbedded in his face. Digging out a red pen, I made scarlet rivulets trickle downward here and there from the point of impact. Big Al's "Award" hung in the maintenance trailer for many days as a reminder of the close call.

Only five days later—during the maintenance break – "Eagle-Eye Al" discovered my turbine engine's diffuser was totally cracked out and just about to ruin my day. (She was running kinda hot.) That was the good news. The bad news was, our poor Boss would have to buy a new engine. We were done!

"There go the Christmas bonuses," Al groaned. This time, I groaned in harmony, as did the whole danged crew when they heard the news. It'll be a lean holiday, now—for sure.

Driving south the next morning for an early Christmas in sunny California, I could at least be thankful for the fact that Big Al had saved my aching butt, once again.

When Turbines Explode!

My Wife Called Me "El Gato."

It was my first day back in my loggin' helicopter following a ten-day break, and I was a bit worried about what I might find (or might not find, in this case) lying on the hillside. I had left over a dozen overweight logs lying there, but they were gone. I deduced in my Okie brain that either a UFO had come along and hoisted them away (for some deranged cellulose experimentation, perhaps) or they had been bucked (recut) and flown to the landing. Or, worst-case scenario, my relief pilot had done what I couldn't do, in this very aircraft. At 7000 feet MSL in the dog days of summer. Yikes!

To put my dilemma in perspective, the average Bell UH-1H can dead-lift 4,000 pounds at sea level on a cool day. More, if the wind is blowing 20 knots or so and the fuel cells hold mostly fumes. More, if you simply toss the operator's manual out the convenient hole in the bubble window; slide your brain into a bell jar; hand the bell jar to the frowning mechanic; and put your spurs on!

Does the term Wenatchee Snatch ring a bell? Not for the faint of heart! I actually had an owner-operator tell me once that a helicopter such as mine could "pull six [thousand] pounds, if you've got the guts." Mondo guts, poquito brains, amigo.

This particular Huey was my favorite. It had been in the capable hands of an ace mechanic, and I trusted him. When it came to matters of go/no-go, "Steve" had always given it to me straight since our first assignment together on an Aerospatiale Lama over 15 years previously.

Steve had a big smile waiting for me when I drove up early that morning, but he quickly relaxed his welcome-face and dropped the other shoe: our Bell's engine was drinking turbine oil! Just under one quart per hour was technically within limits, but the oil was also running darker than usual. I reminded Steve that the big Lycoming had been consuming less than a quart per day when I went on break. Steve also remembered that I had declined to fly the big logs, leaving them for the sawyer to buck up.

Steve had been on the phone to our maintenance chief many miles distant from our central Idaho location, sharing the day-to-day progress of the helicopter's T53-13B engine. The chief assured us that another –13 engine was "in the can and arriving in two days, so watch that oil consumption and keep on loggin'."

Watch the consumption: Unnecessary advice from a guy who flies a desk for a living! The engine started up just fine and the cool morning air was delicious. But the low temps promised to burn away by ten o'clock, and by then we'd be "suckin' mud," as they say. Too hot to be productive. Unless the wind came up, in which case we had a reprieve and could probably get in a complete day of logging, around eight hours of flight time.

As I worked my way through the hooker rotation, taking three or four turns from each man on the fire salvage sale, I knew eventually I'd be coming to 'Hooker Tony,' who had once tied me to the aforementioned logs, back when. Tony was finally 150 feet below the ship, cramming prickly wire-choker eyes into the 80 pound remote hook, sending out beautiful three-to-six log turns. I eventually asked, "Hey, Tony, I see the big pickles made it to the landing, how many did you have to buck?" And to my amazement, he responded, "Not a one, pal! Dick flew all them hogs to the landing."

I'm getting a bad feeling here. Each time I reared back and tried to fly one of those hooters off the ground, the engine gas producer raced to 101.5%, the exhaust gas temp (EGT) needle kissed the red line. Yet all this turning, burning, and lots of body English produced only 38 psi torque. I needed 50 psi to get the big wood up. The rotor rpm quickly drooped, and the heavy turn settled to the ground, a little closer to the log landing—but no cigar. And the wind was blowin' pretty good that day!

"Time for a chain saw," I had advised Tony, and off I clattered in search of turns the aircraft would fly within limits. In order to have the peace of mind necessary to make a living logging with single-engine helicopters, a pilot must believe that his logging-pilot peers—with whom he shares the aircraft—adhere to the same rules that he does. Rule Number One would go something like this: "Keep the damned thing within limits!"

So I had to tell myself that "Dick" was simply a better pilot by getting those oversized beer cans to the log landing.

"Now wait just a danged minute," my Okie brain hollered back at me.

I've been doing this for a while! I probably had around 9000 flight hours by then, and well over half of that was long-line work with heavy loads. I had loaded hundreds of log trucks. I knew the score. A spade was a spade.

The day grew hot as expected, and soon the ol' bird was laboring. A flickering master caution light caught my eye suddenly and I noticed the engine oil pressure gauge needle was a blur. Oil temp was okay, but I called out the problem over the Wulfsberg and headed to the Service LZ, about a half-mile distant, dividing my attention by scanning the panel while searching for a spot to put the bird down. Made it to the LZ and Steve was waiting for me.

After shutdown, Steve pulled the engine oil filter screens and found them to be fairly coked-up. Another call was made to the desk wizard, and based on Steve's description, the wizard directed Steve to blast out the screens with solvent, replace them and run the engine for several minutes, which we did.

"No flickering oil pressure gauge? You're good to go," advised the wizard. Remembering that we all had had some small paychecks recently, back I floundered into the hot sticky air, the 150-foot line dangling between my legs. I made a note to myself at that point that Steve's deodorant was beginning to fade. Check that: it was I.

A little over a half hour later, after gently dropping Mark's last turn at the log landing and radioing "Coming to Tony," there was the flickering oil pressure gauge again. "I've got the problem again," I radioed, "Headin' for Service." I stole a peek at the bubble door panel while I had a second, and the large amber caution light glared back at me. I reset it. It was dark for a second, then came right back on. Not a good sign.

Before I could scan right to verify the problem on the master caution panel, something I'd never seen before caught my eye: the EGT gauge's needle was climbing past the 610 degree Celsius redline, heading straight for the peg.

It was around then that I noticed the distinct odor of burnt oil and a new sound growing in volume behind me, an ominous rumble that made the hair on my neck rise up several degrees. My Okie ancestors were trying to tell me that the durned turbine was about to take a crap.

I keyed the mike again. "I'm gonna have to put her down here." To which the little blonde lady at the log landing responded, "Dorcey, *you're on fire!*"

Now I know she meant well, but I was still two hundred feet in the air, over rough terrain and was trying to sort out the best route around some tall snags and find a place to plant the ship and she had to go and say that.

Punching off the long-line just outside the log-landing perimeter, I hastily descended for the sloping hillside ahead of me—snags, stumps boulders, and all. I'm pleased to tell you that the engine made power all the way to Terra Firma, although she was a'rumblin' and must have looked mucho unairworthy to even the casual observer. The downhill skid barely missed a stump while a boulder kissed the uphill skid. No scratches, no rotor strikes.

So there I was, back on the ground and it was beginning to look like I was gonna make it home to Momma one more time when the little blonde lady radioed, "Get your ASS OUT of that thing, Dorcey! You're on FIRE!"

But I still had hold of a wounded Huey that was inching sideways down the hill. I was in the process of turning the throttle off, likewise the fuel switch and a few more of my favorites but the steepness of the left-skid-low incline was pulling my upper body into the bubble door, making my house-cleaning chores difficult.

Imagine my dismay when, with the throttle rolled to the cut-off position and the fuel switch flipped off, I heard the unmistakable sound of the engine's compressor dramatically sucking air into the intake, the engine RPM began to accelerate toward oblivion!

[Blondie ain't seen nothin' yet.] The rotor system, for all my stuck-wing friends, is mechanically linked with the engine for this mad dash to hell, so I quickly began to fear that main rotor break-up was imminent. I recall involuntarily pulling my head into my shoulders like a turtle as the incredible sound of the out-of-control engine-rotor-system screamed upward to a crescendo that could only end in a violent explosion. Ear plugs, anyone? Kaaaaaaa-BLOOEY!!!

The explosion sent about twenty hookers, cutters, and other woodsmen (mushroom pickers, tree huggers & little blonde ladies) running from a mile around in my direction. I was still getting my harness unbuckled and you probably could have seen hundreds of little question marks hovering over my head like a cartoon as I scrambled out the door and down the hill—taking giant strides— wondering what the heck and relishing the relative quiet of the rotors swirling rapidly behind me. (They were whistling weirdly for some reason.)

Once I had run two hundred feet or so, I spun around to see an oil fire raging on the engine deck while more flames were dripping over the side of the fuselage, catching the paint on fire.

"Grab some fire extinguishers," I called to the landing crew, and I raced back to the ship— thinking how crazy my loyalty to the ship might appear, but I wasn't about to watch this bird burn, not after bringing me safely back to Earth!

In seconds, the ship's little five-pound extinguisher was played out, but just in time came the landing crew—two of them—toting two each, ten-pound Halogen fire bottles, which did the job.

A full five minutes passed as my loggin' buddies came running, swapping expletives and staring in wonder at the football-sized smoking hole atop the burner can where the turbine wheels had exited straight up into the rotor blades.

I was hacking up my third Halogen hairball when I noticed that down between my sneakers and the corked boots belonging to the Woods Boss, a wisp of smoke had just popped out of the forest duff.

The following instant, we were almost run over by a herd of around ten woodsmen lugging backpack water sprayers. A State fire crew was headed uphill, totally ignoring us.

We looked over the tops of their hard hats, past the distorted remains of my engine, the rotor blades pierced completely through numerous times by turbine wheel fragments. Several hundred feet up the hill, smoke was billowing up into the tall Douglas fir. I had started a damned forest fire!

Us downstream boys began stomping out five or more little smokes which had popped up near the Huey in the past few seconds, started by tiny shards of red-hot engine parts.

Then came the water-dropping helicopter. Piloted by none other than the afore-mentioned relief pilot, who happened to be logging with our sister crew nearby. "Dick" had heard the commotion over his Wulfsberg. He and his mechanic did a quick job of converting his K-model Bell from a logging-ship-to-fire-fighter, flying a 300-gallon Bambi bucket down to a deep blue lake only a minute away.

Now Dick was the hero, putting bucket after bucket of cold mountain lake water right on the money, plus a little mist wafting our way to help cool us off. I was feeling the irony of the situation, big time! I looked up and gave him a thanks-now-go-away gesture as he blathered off down the hill. He didn't come back. End of story.

Well, almost: An analysis was months in coming from the desk guy, but common sense and a good friend who really knows his engines had long before determined that the turbine blew a forward internal seal, allowing turbine oil to flood directly into the red hot burner section. The oil rapidly converted into tremendous energy and sped the gas producer and turbine wheels on their way to a catastrophic break-up.

Epilogue: Lucky me! And ever since, I've made a promise to my significant other that I will never, ever fly any helicopter that Dick has so much as leaned up against.

Bigger is Better, Eh?

The Politics of Piloting Large Helicopters

Spread across a humongous tarmac near Fort Rucker many years ago, my fellow Warrant Officer Candidates and I were busy checking the numerous Av-gas fuel sumps on our small-ish Bell TH-13T instrument trainers—all the while admiring a huge, greasy Sikorsky CH-54A Skycrane parked on the nearby wash rack. Four Army crewmen were scrubbing her all over from tall mobile platforms, soaping her clean. Spraying the solvent away with high-pressure hoses created a sporadic rainbow in the morning mist, reminding me of at least one promise made along the bumpy road leading to those coveted silvery wings. The giant-sized Sikorsky represented a good pilot's eternal reward. At least, from where I stood.

The Crane was a new bird in those days, and many of us lowly pilots-in-training had blurry visions of someday climbing up her steps and sliding into the coveted right seat. I say blurry because all of us were headed for Vietnam. Pondering life beyond the nebulous curtain of combat was a thing through which none of us could focus.

Yet, there she sat. Massive beyond anything we'd ever seen that had rotor blades welded to it, temporarily paralyzing my hapless WOC buddies and me. Blissfully unaware of the nefarious flight instructor sneaking up behind me. Lechery and intimidation were at hand. Braced for ogling when I should have been pre-flighting, I assumed the position and began pushing Alabama away from myself: "One, Sir! Two, Sir! Three, Sir!" (Etc. ad infinitim).

In the time that followed, I was fortunate to survive The 'Nam—and afterward, I logged time in several Army Hueys, the round-motored

"Choctaw" (Sikorsky H-34); got some serious stick time in De Havilland Beavers and Otters – (I missed flying a real live twin round-motored H-37 Mojave by a couple of days.)

Like most young pilots, I was programmed to covet the big stuff. However, I couldn't help but notice that—once the novelty wore off—my fun meter didn't go up in proportion with rotor diameter. And I wondered why.

All too often a pilot looking for a seat in a multi-crew aircraft is faced with adversity of one kind or another. Having a commercial rotorcraft ticket, multiengine time, and several thousand hours Pilot in Command gets you precisely nowhere unless you've done penance somewhere, paid your dues, and/or kissed mondo hiney.

One ex-logging outfit I am familiar with dictated that no one would fly their Cranes unless they first rose to Captain in the Bell 214. "The way to the Crane is thru the 214!" I can still hear the Chief Pilot pontificating.

My finances at the time were such that I needed a Skycrane Captain's logging salary to stay afloat, so I ignored all the horror stories and statistics and focused on slingin' them six thousand pound logs along under one engine and two big, fat rotors for another year or two.

And during that span of time, a miracle happened. One of my logging pilot peers who simply refused to go loggin' in the Bell 214B was given a seat in the Crane. The secret code had somehow been cracked! (I couldn't help but notice that he and the Chief Pilot smoked the same brand; surely that had nothing to do with the *immaculate exception*.)

Then one day I got the long-awaited call. "I've got a Crane seat for you," his silvery tongue slathered, "but your Crane is waiting for some work. If you want any flight pay, you might wanna keep loggin' in the 214."

A few months went by. On a hot June afternoon my brand new wireless phone abruptly began to chortle. It was none other than ol' Silver Tongue with bad news. The Outfit had folded!

"Nobody has a job," ol' Silver Tongue would have me believe. Lots of folks, including yours truly, were suddenly unemployed and owed money. Another theoretical neon rainbow vaporized against the hot California sky as I mashed down hard on the plastic button, killing the annoying flow of data.

Then came depression, bankruptcy, and wildfire. Devastating fires swept the steeply forested mountains of central Washington State. I was sweltering under the air conditioner when that worrisome telephone warbled once again: An all-too-familiar Crane operator (sporting a new shingle) invited me to fly to Wenatchee, WA to help crew his CH-54A on a *project* fire. Meaning *big!*

In exchange for a month of my time, a promise was made: "Come on up and we'll get you checked out and carded in the Crane." That was music to my ears, because the roof was leaking, the bulldog was gnawing on my leg bone, and Repo Man had his hooks on the Bentley. [Make that…Ford.]

In a subsequent call, the Chief Pilot cheerfully agreed to make a copy of the "Dash 10" (operator's manual) available for much study time ahead. (A thorough Crane oral exam could last two hours.) I hastily packed a bag, attached the bulldog to my tearful wife's leg bone, and headed north.

Once in (smoky) Washington, a frowning mob of familiar faces gathered around the fuel tanker's twin jet trailers. Most were smoking cigarettes like a herd of tar-sucking nicotine fiends. I was disappointed to discover that yours truly was one of the few non-smokers in the whole outfit! This made for surreal "Safety Meetings," and long, nauseating rides in the crew rigs.

No one seemed to care if I needed to breathe or not. In between gasps for oxygen, I asked the Chief Pilot for that "spare" Dash 10 so I could begin studying for my S-64 Oral. With a straight face, I was informed there was only one – it was in the ship – "Just don't remove it from the aircraft," he added — drowning his butt in a convenient Styrofoam coffee cup, which was reeking with countless soggy predecessors. My study periods were reduced to rare stops and periods of darkness.

Following the usual Forest Service hazard/safety orientation, I was introduced to the Crane's jump seat – back behind the two-man flight crew, but up and forward of the rear-facing pilot's position. I committed the lengthy starting procedure to memory, following the front-seaters down the endless list. Multiple everything, no ashtrays.

Soon her nine thousand horses were beginning to lather. The Captain bid her upward, and we churned ahead toward the assignment, dangling the 2,000-gallon Bambi bucket well below us. I looked over my shoulder—there was an amazing view behind me—but a frustrating, horizon-less view forward.

It was honestly a pain to endure two hours and forty-five minutes of ceaseless bobbing and chain-smoking while the Guys Up Front blatantly ignored an N1 surging problem on the number two engine. Didn't seem to faze them, though—as they long-lined the Bambi bucket around in the nebulous haze, "making seven thousand dollars an hour," I heard more than once.

(Right about then, I began to speculate: If that surging engine problem don't get me, the second- hand smoke will!)

Over the next few days—ignoring all the little signals that I should return to safer skies – I gravitated to the right seat and began to put in six-hour days. We were crewing the ship with four pilots in two shifts—which was nice—except that I could rarely study the Dash 10. Another non-rated right-seater pilot had his own copy, somehow, and was about to take his Oral exam. Had to be coincidental that he and the Chief Pilot were motel roommates and smoked the same brand of cigarettes. *Had to be.*

Things around the project fire were getting hairy. In the thick morning smoke, three Cranes and two S-61s hovered along low level in and out of one drainage or another, Division Alpha over to Division Bravo, down to Division X-Ray, you get the picture.

The other two Cranes had the new snorkel rigs with thirty-five foot hoses. Ours had the original Skycrane hoist installed, so we wound the Bambi bucket up and down on a thick, one-hundred-foot braided steel cable when the visibility was low and we had to feel our way along.

On the positive side, the bucket work was rather spectacular. We were dipping from moss-infested circular ponds, deep mountain lakes, and swirling pools along the abundant white-water rivers. On endless fire lines we repeatedly knocked down walls of flaming timber in an otherwise hopeless attack on the relentless inferno.

I tried hard to be a good, loyal right-seater, but the prevailing cockpit ventilation worked against me. The Captain's logging bubble had a hole cut in the bottom. The air flowed inward through that opening, picked up his Marlboro fall-out and carried it over to my right-hand window, which was always hinged open. Smoke had to pass under my sensitive nose on the way out. A constant smoke-out.

One day I flew right seat with one of the owners, and old friend. He was clearly relieved to be making money, but he didn't seem to be too excited about flying the big iron. He confessed in a weak moment, "A Huey's a lot more fun than flyin' one of these things." Frowning had creased his face over the years, I noted.

(My thoughts returned to my late bosses' words on the subject: Floyd Hiser had no frown lines, and he knew the score: "We work to have fun, and to make money.")

About the time Ol' Silver Tongue concluded that we were indispensable, the Forest Service released our Crane to a fire in northwestern Montana, near the Canadian border. "No heavies on that one," he said, "everyone is screaming for resources!" Naturally, when I landed the Crane at our destination, there was a long line of idle Cranes and Vertols basking in the hot sun. Their pilots were just sitting there—sucking up all the ice-cold apple juice that could be trucked into Fire Camp.

Within a few hours, we were farmed out to yet another fire. The following day I got a few hours off to study the ship's Dash 10 when the Outfit's A-Team "lost" the Bambi bucket while dipping from a pristine mountain pond. Wear and tear from hoisting the bucket up and down had caused an electrical arc, triggering the bucket's release. We were AOG.

A special team of divers had to be called in. The following morning, vivid, grim descriptions were relayed from the divers' boat concerning a ten-foot thick accumulation of ancient ducky-do on the pond's bottom, in which Bambi was mired.

The gallant divers sank to the occasion, however, and we were soon hooked up to the completely full, non-deployable bucket – followed by a slow, harrowing flight at max "eepers" to slosh the excessive ducky-do and water out of the bucket along the opposite shoreline, lightening the load. We then lumbered over to the fire's main helibase to repair the bucket.

Once back in service, we fell into a familiar routine: After "wheels down" from a fire-fighting cycle, a junior mechanic would trot over during hot-refuel with a bench brush and dustpan. As one pilot headed for the little blue building, the rookie A&P's first order of business was to sweep that big pile of butts out from under the left seat, where the Crane Driver of the Cycle would crush 'em out – right on Igor's precious cockpit floor. One would think—for seven thousand bucks an hour—they could at least afford an empty tin can with some sand in it.

Done for the day, I stuffed my sweaty flight helmet into its drab bag. Standing in the shade of the beast, I scanned the horizon for the illusive rainbow, but saw only more smoke and some mean lookin' cumulonimbus. And that little orange dot, low in the sky, yonder. Growing larger all the time.

An interesting re-crossing of paths was about to occur: Over the vacant meadow East of us, a brand-new lookin' S-64E approached—blocking out the sun with its daunting, Praying Mantis form—causing utter chaos around her until she finally throttled down to flight idle. After the APU shut down, I ambled over to check out the latest version of the legendary Tarhe.

Walking under the lofty, seventy-two foot, six-main-rotor-bladed behemoth, did I see a face I recognized? Sure enough, it was a tall lanky guy who turned wrenches years ago in Rialto. He had bounced around awhile afterward, gaining flight experience. "Tall Guy" eventually returned to work for his original outfit—one of the better-known large helicopter operators on Planet Earth. Now he was busy flying E Models and fighting fires all over the planet. The semi-permanent frown on his face turned into a smug expression when he recognized me.

"Hey, Wingo, what's up?" he said, extending his hand. I replied, "Howdy," and explained that I was with "Brand X, yonder" – nodding my head in the direction of the old, ex-military machine. "Trying to make some house payments, mostly," I must have sounded apologetic.

That loosened his tongue up a bit, and he was soon giving me the royal tour of an Echo Model. Many improvements, mostly hidden. The comparisons were noteworthy, as some serious re-engineering was done to make her stronger, fly smoother, lift more—and talk to the crew in a calm, sexy female voice! (Nice touch, Igor!)

Standing next to the snorkel's killer hydraulic suction pump, the very man who helped design the system (just recently certified) proudly gave me a quick class on the design. "It's bullet proof. It will suck up two thousand gallons of water—or mud—in under one minute, if that's all there is."

(Professional mud suckers?...My cartoonist brain wriggled...I smelled a story!) Eventually, my tall guide and I walked to a quieter place under yon shade tree.

I confessed that my tour with Brand X was coming to an end and that I was (once again) looking for work. Tall Guy tried not to act too amused by a question he must have heard a lot. He explained that his Captain's seats were all filled, thanks – "We'll let you know."

And just as Tall Guy ran out of nice things to say, a brand new, six-wheeled field support truck bearing a familiar magnetic icon on its door rumbled down the dirt road toward us, flashing his headlights. Tall Guy pretended the rare signal meant nothing, going on to say that he was "really worried" about the influx of military surplus Cranes. With a disapproving glance toward our old Tarhe, he concluded:

"I just hope these guys don't embarrass us!" (Us, meaning the Standard Category Skycrane operators.)

When the beefy, air-conditioned truck pulled up, an urgent look on the seasoned driver's face told Tall Guy to climb in and shut the door. I took the hint. Shaking my proud guide's hand, I split. As I walked toward my waiting crew truck, I wondered if Tall Guy knew more about Brand X than he was willing to say, or if his thoughts were mere idle speculation.

Within minutes, word spread all around Fire Camp and over the horizon: Tall Guy's sister ship had hover-sucked itself into a gross-overload situation while snorkeling over a lake just north of us. The highly advanced, well-financed machine settled like a flailing Cyclops into the cold, deep water.

The shocked flight crew had to swim over a quarter mile to shore – flight helmets, Nomex suits, leather boots, and ducky-do – get the picture?

A certain Okie I resemble was left to wonder at that point: Who among us was having fun; who was embarrassed, and who was just blowin' smoke?

Primary flight training—Fort Wolters, Texas—June, 1968.

GOODBYE DRIVE SHAFT, HELLO TREES!

"This is gonna be ugly, boys!" I radioed my logging crew.

One of the most significant improvements that you as an operator can make on a Bell UH-1 series helicopter is to remove the standard engine-to-transmission drive shaft ("short shaft") and throw it just as far as you can! The darned thing doesn't hold a candle to the Kaman Ka-Flex drive shaft as a retrofit: Tough as nails, yet flexible, which makes all the difference in the world when you're working the machine hard. Charlie makes a winner.

Even so, the Ka-Flex can fail, and of all the nasty problems a chopper pilot can experience, this one rates way up there. Especially on the Huey, because when it fails, it usually doesn't let go all at once. Which is nice, but in failing, any broken links literally shred the thin sheet metal air intake housing surrounding it. This, in turn, is ingested directly and with prejudice into the Lycoming engine's compressor section just aft of the shaft. All this makes for FOD with a capital "F." So even if the shaft doesn't fail right away, the engine is on its way out. Ya gotta get it on the ground. Now you know.

Which brings us, gentle readers, to early dawn near the little town of Addy, Washington, not long ago. I was flexing my creaky neck and performing my routine preflight inspection by flashlight.

The month of June has to be the glory month for this part of the country, and the helicopter logging had been going great. I had the pleasure of working with a very talented and attentive mechanic, an old friend from the days when we both had hair.

Gaylord was waiting patiently for me to climb down and get on with my flying, but he knows I'll regularly climb up on the ship and get greasy like a good loggin' pilot should. Everything looked groovy, I noted. Spinning the Ka-Flex around to the right and shining the light here and there, I watched the pinkish glow to the east out of the corner of one eye so I didn't keep my logging crew waiting in the woods.

"Well, all the big pieces are here. Let's light this puppy!" I quipped. Ambling down the step-holes, I swung into the left-hand driver's seat. Gaylord obliged me with an APU start and soon I was headed into the pine-scented air while Gaylord headed for the coffee-pot.

Everything was going along slicker than deer guts on a brass doorknob up until the elapsed timer hit the thirty-minute mark. I was headed uphill and eastbound, dangling the 150-foot long-line along with an empty remote hook at 80 knots. I had just called out "Comin' to Brian," when the Ka-Flex suddenly let go. I flinched involuntarily at the sudden loud buzz-saw noise and accompanying vibration. For a second I felt very small and unprepared. I knew right away, it had to be the shaft.

Reducing power and punching off the line, I tried to announce my problem over the radio calmly, but I think my message went out an octave higher than usual, "I've got a PROBLEM!" Brian didn't hear me, I reckon, 'cause he came right back on the radio describing his load of logs and how I should go about pulling it all together. I was about to reassert my situation when another hooker yelled over his remote microphone, "Shuddup, Brian, he's got a problem!"

I announced the problem as a "drive shaft," and that I was looking for a place to land. I knew there were no LZs anywhere in the unit; just steep hillsides and 140-foot tall trees, and getting taller all the time.

I saw one of my "hookers" in a tiny clearing surrounded by big Larch trees ahead of me and up the hill, but if I tried to squeeze in there, I'd send rotor blade chunks flying everywhere – not an option! Downhill to the right I clattered, the buzzing bedlam relentless and intimidating. The dual tachometer was reading in the green, a welcomed sight, but I knew that time was running out.

I couldn't help but notice the farther downhill I went the taller and more pointy the Larch trees appeared, and I tried not to think about how they were going to feel when I came down vertically right on top of 'em, blue jeans and BVDs or no. I was still holding 55 knots but wanting desperately to slow down for the impending impact.

Down below me, I caught a glimpse of a 4X4 logging trail through the trees and told myself to go ahead, take what I had and chop my way on down when I noticed Dan Medina, the Project Manager was right under me, climbing out of his truck. Nuts.

With airspeed down to around forty-five knots and the trees close enough to read their bar codes, I heard the last remnants of the Ka-Flex going bye-bye. Which sounded a lot like those tin cans dingling along behind my Mercury when I got married. Then things got a lot quieter, which any chopper pilot knows, is not a good thing.

The engine was spooling down, killed by FOD. I rolled off the throttle, involuntarily tightening my sphincter in preparation to set 'er down on a humongous Tamarack directly in front of me!

I decided it was time to say goodbye to my crew at this point, radioing "This is gonna be ugly, boys." Just then I spotted a narrow dirt road coming into view through the branches ahead of me, a beautiful sight!

Using what precious little maneuverable energy was left in the rotor system, I flared enough to slide over the tree top, dropped the pitch and made a slight right hand turn to line up with the road. I was seeing everything in slow motion about then, several 30-foot trees along the left side of the road would be the first to impact the rotors, the steep incline above the road would take out what was left.

Something made me take one last look at the rotor tach, the blades were turning so slowly I was amazed the ship was responding as well as it did: 170 RPM! That's flight idle, sports fans; about half the RPM we are so fond of flying with. Gravity was in control.

The rest was pretty much academic: the trees were being severed, the ship turning right as I pulled what was left on the collective, easing back on the cyclic to hit with as little forward speed as possible and bracing for the main rotor's impact with the hillside to my right.

It was ugly! After taking out the trees, vertical impact broke off the tail boom like a big one-time-only shock absorber, and the forty-eight-foot rotor system shattered against Mother Earth. The nose of the chopper came down hard, digging into the ground for a brief slide, during which time yours truly was bounced headfirst through the green house window above the left seat. (Seatbelt? You betcha! Bruises? Comin' right up.)

And then the quiet. I hit the ground a-runnin,' delighted to see my legs doing so well under me, realizing too late that I had forgotten to unplug my helmet cord from the ship's female adapter, and recoiling from the "POP" I got when I ran out of cord. Damn.

Looking back, flames were coming from the exhaust stack, and I didn't waste much time running back to put them out. In doing so, I got a good look at the tangled spaghetti that used to be my Ka-Flex: Toast.

As all the mosquitoes in eastern Washington began draining me of my Type-O (for Okie?) blood, I realized that my creaky neck—a bane to many long-line pilots—felt all warm and tingly, like I'd just been to the chiropractor.

And then the boys began popping out of the trees above the scene, hot and sweaty, all out of breath they scrambled down the steep hillside to help save me from all them 'skeeters. Grinning from ear to ear, I had but one thought: Life was good.

Plan "B" From Outer Montana

Winter's hold on our Huey was about to be tested!

"Life is a bowl of cherries," some optimist once said, long before helicopters began chopping up the morning mist. Lots of optimists become airplane pilots—only a few become helicopter pilots—or mechanics, for that matter. The comparatively high cost of learning to fly a chopper is one barrier facing the optimist status quo. For the financially deprived young optimist—who wants it really bad—the military is an option that cannot be ignored. (Snip goes the ponytail.)

Optimism is frowned upon in the training helicopter's cockpit, it is soon learned. "I'll beat it into your thick skull with a #%*&$! baseball bat, if that's what it takes," my stressed-out flight instructor once verbalized to me. Some of the spit generated by his staccato alliteration stopped short of my sweaty face, thanks to my G.I. Ray-Bans.

Mr. Wells was hammering home the finer points of lowering the collective if-and-when he chopped the throttle on our Hiller, an OH-23D Raven. The successful outcome of an emergency landing depended upon spontaneous reflex—and a few other tricks that kicked in a little closer to the ground.

I was in complete agreement, of course. And from his point of view, the spit on my brand new shades spelled out, "Yesss Sirrr!!" Only when his fundamental training took hold was I allowed the privilege of feeling optimistic again—so long as our skids were no more than three feet off the ground.

As it turns out, optimism can be a dangerous thing, even with one's skids on the ground. It tends to replace the lessons we learned from the older pilots and from white-knuckled experiences. Given too much rein, optimism displaces caution and overtakes common sense. An ugly scene on a cool spring morning comes to mind.

Holding herd as the Chief Pilot over two Montana-based logging Hueys was, for an adrenaline junky, a truly great job. But that year's winter was particularly hard; half of our logs got buried in the crotch-deep snow. Parlez vous Lay-off? One of the Hueys had to be parked and stored in the old gravel quarry, right next to her sister ship's service landing. Lorena—we called her— arrived late the next day from Paradise, without its winter covers. Someone spaced the covers on the long list of things to do.

When I noticed that Lorena was tied down with no rotor blade, head, or engine shroud covers, I casually mentioned it to the local mechanic, "Big Al." I hinted that maybe somebody should come up with some makeshift covers. Al displayed his ever-present grin—which was surrounded by a large herd of freckles—and mumbled something about a plan he had.

Having contributed my two cents worth, I merrily went about my winter loggin'routine in "Blue Duck," the smoother flying of the two birds. As always, Big Al saluted as I pulled away vertically, then bee-lined for his cozy camper as my remote hook lurched into the crisp mountain air, 185 feet below.

In the weeks that followed, one snow-and-ice-storm after another plastered western Montana. Poor old Lorena was soon part of a snow bank and in the grip of dirty, blue ice. Frequently blasted by Blue Duck's rotor wash, Lorena shivered in a month-long shadow cast by the high ridge just south of us. The low-angled sun's rays seldom touched her corner of the quarry.

Between storms, someone tossed a battered-and-burnt, blue plastic tarp over Lorena's transmission and part of the engine deck. But between Blue Duck's rotor-wash and the relentless Montana weather, Lorena became a billboard for neglect. The old blue tarp looked pitiful—all tattered and wrapped around the mast—under layers of ice. Her rotor head and droopy rotor blades were locked down by the icy hand of winter. I thought about photographing her in that shameful state, but things were getting kind of dicey around our little operation, so I decided against tossing any sodium chloride into the gaping wound.

And then it happened. A big thaw came in the early spring, and both birds were given the green light to start logging.

Big Al came to a three-foot hover and began firing up all his space heaters to warm up Lorena. Two hours later, I noticed that her cabin was almost defrosted, but nothing much had changed on the high steel. Al occasionally pried at the blue tarp; it was giving way in small sections.

This plan of attack didn't look like it was really going to work, so I suggested throwing a big tarp over the whole blade assembly. That would trap the hot air rising from the kerosene heaters and thaw the stubborn ice.

But Big Al was optimistic that his plan was going to work, so I stood aside and let the man do his thing. He was soon up on his ten-foot ladder, persuading chunks of ice to slide off the sweating rotor blades. "When we crank, the rest of this stuff will slough right off," he forecasted.

Big Al had already summoned an old friend of mine to come start the beast. "Dave" was a high-time Vietnam veteran and our on-call relief pilot. He looked kinda like "Fred Mertz" of the old *I Love Lucy Show*, and he kept his bald head under a baseball cap to keep from freezing his brain. Al had prepped Dave as to the progress of the de-icing operation and confidently predicted that the ship would be ready to crank in an hour or so.

Yours truly went loggin' just up the canyon in Blue Duck while Al and Dave looked Lorena over. Pulling pitch, I could see Dave holding his cap down with one hand while staring squinty-eyed at the ice-clad steel above Lorena's transmission. He was standing close to a cherry-red space heater attempting to keep warm, and my blustery departure didn't help much. Al had the APU warming up and was looking toward the sun for help.

Sure enough, one hour and twenty-five minutes later I was back on the gravel pad for another cycle's worth of jet fuel—and to stretch my legs. "Fatty," our Party Manager, was on hand to hot-fuel the Duck as I jotted down the data from the logging computer, calculating the turns-per-hour and average weight per turn.

Looking up from my knee-pad, I noticed Big Al standing between the Duck and Lorena. He was grinning—of course—giving me the old twirling finger sign. Dave was about to crank 'er up.

Lorena sat in a vast mud puddle, half in the bright morning sun, half in the cold gray shadows as her optimistic pilot mashed on the start button. Mr. Lycoming was just starting to whistle loudly as the melting ice on the rotor blades began to rain in slowly accelerating circles. Al watched, shocked to observe one of Lorena's main rotor blades suddenly shed its heavy load of ice off to her left front, smashing into the nearby jet fuel tractor-trailer with a great <u>WHUMP</u>!!!

Fortunately for Al, Blue Duck, and the tanker, the other rotor blade's load of ice decided to stay right where it was. Unfortunately for Lorena and Dave—and those of us who had to watch the ugliest thing that could possibly happen to a Huey without killing it: The heavier blade created such an extreme lateral out-of-balance situation that the ship had no choice but lean hard toward it as she was yanked around by the icy mass orbiting crazily around her. Her nose dipped low, leaned left, climbed, leaned right, dipped again while her skids twisted and groaned—her mast was clobbered time and again by the teetering rotor head, sounds of rivets popping like rifle shots echoed around the quarry.

Meanwhile, Dave had long since aborted the start sequence and was holding on to the cyclic for dear life. I could see that he had lost his cap and that he had no seat belt on by the way Lorena was using him to wipe out the cockpit. Al stood frozen in his snow boots; the perennial optimistic expression was gone. It was replaced by he-who-shoots-self-in-foot.

It seemed to take forever for the thrashing to stop. Lucky that nothing had hit the Duck, I sighed and rolled off her throttle. Time to reduce the confusion and check for damage. Big Al silently dragged a brand new tarp out of the maintenance trailer. Up and over the rotor head it went, and soon Lorena's icy rotor blade was getting the suggested heat treatment. A certain relief pilot was visibly shook up and embarrassed. A freckled mechanic wished he had the morning to do all over again.

After watching our two grown optimists crank up such a spectacle, I only had a couple of things to say about it: "No seatbelt, Dave? Kinda' hard to turn off the switches when you're being thrown all over the cockpit, ain't it?" And to Big Al: "That was the ugliest thing I've seen in a long, long time."

Loggin' in the Spring—2001.

A&P Mechanic Joe Hendrik refuels Blue Duck in the Little Joe River drainage, while the hookers shiver!

More Adventures Under the Twirling Rotors

DEAD-EYE LYLE and the SONS of the CODE TALKERS

Firefighting in Navajo Country

Of all the fire-related helicopter work that I've had the pleasure of being paid to fly, very near the top must be those three choice summers I shared with my Native American friends on the Navajo Reservation. This was in the mid-1980s.

The three-year BIA contract specs called for the likes of a Hughes (MD) 500D or a Bell 206B III, humble machines in terms of payload, but in the '80s, these birds ruled the roost among the five-place turbine powered helicopters. Western Helicopters operated several models, so we responded with either/or depending on what was available each June.

The contract work period lasted a brief 60 days, beginning with the ubiquitous thunderstorms of summer and ending with the soaking monsoons of late July. In between lay the joys of summer: Thunder storms. Lightning. Wildfires. Water bucket drops. Smoky flight suits. Shoot-outs with real Indians. (Gimme time, I'll get around to that, most skosh.)

Window Rock sits high up along the northeast boundary of Arizona/New Mexico and is the capitol of the Navajo Nation. Each June we'd gear up a ship, a one-ton service/tanker truck, and head east from our California base. We hired our service truck drivers from the local Navajo populace. Our A&P mechanics were "on call," flying out in a stuck-winger as needed.

As Western's director of operations, I usually made the call as to who piloted the ship, and I frequently penned myself in for a share of the fun. My faithful Mexicana wife, Lourdes, called all this frequent absenteeism "Wingo Rock."

And none other than my buddy, Pete Gillies, flew relief. He and his angelic wife Patty and their two young sons settled into a 40-foot trailer near the airport. Few fire contracts "fit" like this little low bidder, a fact not lost on the Gillies.

The Helitack crew was all Navajo and based their operation at the Window Rock Airport, a lofty 6,742 feet MSL. The pilot routinely arrives around 08:30 to preflight the aircraft, prepare the load calculation form, and be ready for launch in the event of a fire call. The MD 500D required an external basket for fire fighting gear, personnel packs, and the occasional rifle or two. (Most skosh.)

(Incidentally, in preparing to man this contract for the first time, I telephoned the previous year's helicopter contractor and asked the owner if he had any advice for us as I packed my flight bag with one hand, and he said, "Damn right I do. Let the Indians run the show. Last thing they want is an outsider to try and run things.")

"No problemo," I responded. Five generations removed from a full-blooded Cherokee, I would fit right in with my Native American brothers. No "bilaganas" on this crew.

A crew of three fire fighters—plus pilot—traditionally made a "recon flight" around the Nation every morning if there was no on-going fire activity, and I learned to anticipate this daily procedure with mixed emotions: I loved the job and the flying, but I learned quickly that low-level turbulence was built-in to this recon, like it or not. The 500's rotor blades would be growling the entire flight.

On one memorable day well into July, we loaded up our three-Indian-crew plus pilot, and brought the Allison 250-C20B gas turbine engine up to 100%. Sliding along the narrow taxiway and gaining a foot in altitude, I strained to stay "on the cushion" and keep the turbine temp in the yellow. The ship lurched into the air as we passed through twenty knots, climbing steadily. Our Patrol Flights always started with a stimulating max-gross takeoff from the airport.

"Dispatch, Patrol 66 Foxtrot. Skids off the ground at ten hundred hours, departing Window Rock Airport," our team leader, Lyle, radioed Fire Dispatch. 'And seat belts extra snug,' I mumbled to myself, anticipating the rocks in the road ahead.

Climbing to the west, I glanced right past Lyle as my eyes were drawn to countless American flags fluttering down in the Window Rock cemetery. Perhaps nowhere in the whole US of A was there a greater enlistment effort to fight in World War II than here on this Reservation. History has recorded that they fought with uncommon valor, among them the famous "Code Talkers" who confounded the Imperialist Japanese with their Navajo crypto.

I flew combat choppers in the 'Nam. Proud to be flying now with the Sons of the Code Talkers! West we patrolled to the edge of the broad green mesa, dotted with Ponderosa pine, Juniper and Pinion. Cumulus clouds building to the southwest. Thunderstorms possible, according to the weather guy. Looking for smoke. Keep looking for smoke.

Minutes later we turned northerly toward Fluted Rock, an ancient elevated black table-top lava flow, complete with a manned fire observation tower. Continuing north, we would begin to feel the wrath of the choppy air over the tourist Mecca known as Canyon De Chelly, home to ancient cliff dwellings (among them, the "White House") and winding canyons punctuated with rare needle-like pinnacles. And once frequented by Kit Carson, to the lament of the 19th century Navajos.

The infamous Trail of Tears began here, and more than one massacre of these Native Americans was shamefully documented in the history books I'd been reading in my motel room at night. I think the Navajo crew recognized my awareness, and a bond developed between us over the term of three years that I cherished and nurtured, leaving me feeling that I must be more Indian than biligana.

As we buzzed along at eighty knots, I tried to size-up my right seat guy. Lyle hadn't been assigned the Team Leader position before. He was a bit older than the rest of the crew, and I noticed from Day One that the crew listened to him. There was something about this wiry Navajo that reminded me of "Blue Duck," the villainous renegade depicted in McMurtry's *Lonesome Dove*, minus the pig-sticker.

Lyle acted friendly enough, when it was called for, but I think it was those *ojos* of his that stirred my wariness. That look, plus a well-circulated account of his alleged romp along the early morning sidewalks of a nearby New Mexican community aboard a powerful dirt bike. Hell's-bells, Lyle lived large, Blue Duck was fiction!

"Dispatch, Patrol 66 Foxtrot. Comin' up on Black Rock, headin' for Roof Butte." Lyle handled the radio well, almost as an afterthought.

He caught me beady-eyeing him and I promptly redirected my gaze forward. I grinned my most brotherly grin and, looking straight ahead, kept pedaling. I was wondering if any of Lyle's ancestors had anything to do with "Bad Day at Black Rock." Damned if I was gonna ask.

Off to our left was none other than Monument Valley, bastion of spectacular pillars and the familiar "mittens," over fifty miles away. Breathtaking. No smokes yonder, neither. Sandstone stands up just fine to fire.

Roof Butte demanded a steady climb to over ten thousand feet, so we started early and pedaled hard. Fifteen minutes later we crested the high ridge that was obscuring the view until now, and there before us stood three absolute gems along the northeastern sector of the Reservation: Roof Butte, Beautiful Mountain, and in the distance, Shiprock! A splendid ancient wind-swept volcano, Shiprock had for many years been to me a polarizing earthly attraction: Ominous, stark, surrealistic, and uniquely serpentine where linear volcanic vents cooled into a long twisting black snake. Eagles and helicopter crews have the best point of view.

(Nine years previously, I had spent an unauthorized night camped out just below Shiprock's monolithic vertical walls facing Farmington. My friendly tent-mate and I warmed a tin of soup over glowing cow chips among the volcanic rocks and sage brush. I felt besieged by the "Winged Rock's" spirit that evening, sensing that *Tse Bit a i* was annoyed by my impertinence. A pickup truck that had followed my VW van that night up to the low shoulders of Shiprock was gone.

At length, the sun peeked over the eastern horizon, and we made my escape before the reinforcements arrived. I couldn't help myself: Spending a night at Shiprock was on my must-do list!)

Ten thousand feet, cool forest air, straining rotors, no smoke. We slide down the east side of Roof Butte to get a good look at Beautiful Mountain and the valley between which is hidden from the lookouts. Down the backstretch to Washington Pass, where we would land if the risk of fire was high. At 9200 feet we would be poised strategically in the center of the prevailing storm cloud path. Today, we were "GO" for standby at Washington Pass.

I turned my concentration now to the tricky landing ahead of us: Checking the wind speed and direction for the turn to final approach. She was blowing lightly right up the pipe—perfect! Squirming my butt into a comfortable spot and enjoying the heck out every second of the approach. The little LZ appeared to our twelve o'clock low, growing steadily.

Our shallow, powered-up approach, required keeping the ship's airspeed above translational lift, then cushioning the flight into a smooth in-ground-effect hover. At last…I eased her on down to earth, like a magic carpet ride. (Or a Navajo blanket, in this case.) Checking my three o'clock: Lyle is grinning like the Cheshire Cat. This Duck loves to fly.

Rotor blades tied down, Curtis Bitsee refuels us to the 1.5 hour level with his finest vintage Jet-A1. Postflight check complete, new load calculation signed off. Now it's time to relax and let the Hopi homeland to our west cook up the distant juicy Cumulus into Nimbus. We unwrap the rifles. And head for the shooting range.

That's right. We fine, upstanding Americans used a portion of our standby time at the Pass by sharpening our shooting skills 'round back of the helispot. There was an old junkyard just over the little ridge, out of sight, and safe as can be.

This is where yours truly pulled a sneaky and extracted two letter-sized plywood targets out of the ship's tiny baggage compartment. Pellet rifle and targets in hand, I followed the Indians up the ridge toward the dump. Lyle's portable radio made squelching noises, early precursors of distant lightning activity.

This wasn't your ordinary pellet rifle I was toting. This was a Sheridan, a spendy little .20 caliber single-shot pump. Conventional blade sights, lots of power, and very accurate. Hardly a scratch on it. This was its first trip to the Pass.

I leaned the unloaded rifle against a stump and walked downrange to set up my targets. Just ahead, my brothers were returning to the stump from setting up a few bottles and cans.

They stopped in their tracks when they noticed me coming with the hand-drawn target boards: One was a caricature of a goofy looking old cowboy, ten-gallon hat and all. The other, my friends, was a caricature of a fierce looking Indian Chief, complete with a huge war bonnet! The cowboy drew lots of laughs; the jury is still out the Chief. Lyle pointed in the direction of the Cowboy. "He's gonna get his," he said, matter-of-factly.

'Long about then I began to wonder if maybe I had carried this culture-differential bit a little too far, cause I was planning' on shootin' the Chief, being the only part-biligana at the firing-range. I wasn't too worried, cause my competition had never fired the Sheridan. I considered myself a crack shooter with it.

Back at the stump, I was showing Curtis how to open the bolt, insert the pellet, pump the air charge up, where the safety was, and all that noise, when Lyle walked over and—without saying a word—gently took the piece from my hands. He turned downrange, lifted the ready-to-fire rifle's walnut stock to his right cheekbone in a classic standing position. And from a distance of over fifty feet Lyle drilled that ignorant looking' Cowboy right between the eyes.

I couldn't believe it. The rest of the crew was whooping like a war party of scalpers as I walked (slowly, alone) downrange to gaze upon Lyle's victim: Bull's eye! "Cowboy, meet Lyle," I mumbled, and returned to the stump and all the grinning Indians gathered 'round it.

Resolutely, I re-loaded the chamber, pumped the Sheridan seven long hard strokes, and raised the barrel. I drew a bead on the Chief. Then came the flash!

A loud crack of thunder spared me the immediate outcome of this lopsided shooting match, a clap so loud and sharp I flinched and almost fired! We spun as a unit toward the sound and saw a fine thunderhead billowing to our west. No sooner did we register the close proximity of the stroke, Black Rock observation tower reported over our portable radio, "Dispatch, lightning strike and smoke observed, vicinity of Washington Pass. I'm leavin' the tower now for safety!"

"Load up," Lyle said, as I sent the pellet flying into a more deserving empty Spam can, relieved to have my skill check put on hold.

Within a minute, the blades were buzzing above us. Were we actually going to see some smoke?! Inching up the collective pitch control with my left hand while nudging the cyclic forward with the right, we began our flight into the thin mountain air like a proverbial lead sled. Lyle lit up the radio with his departure call, announcing, "Dispatch, 66 Foxtrot en route to the scene."

In seconds we were above treetop level, and we could already see the smoke. In what had to be one of the shortest helitack flights ever to a fire scene, we immediately began leveling off and turning slightly to put Lyle in the best position to do a Situation Report. What a sight it was!

Orbiting lazily around to the right, Lyle's Nomex flight suit was flapping merrily and he looked like a man on a mission. Clutching the radio transmitter switch in his left hand, he articulated in plain English what was transpiring in the lush meadow below:

"Dispatch, 66 Foxtrot is on the scene of the smoke, one quarter mile west north west of Washington Pass. Lightning strike. A large standing Ponderosa pine snag. The fire is of low intensity, a few pine shards burning nearby in light fuel. No roads for pumper truck access. We're gonna land and take action, over."

"Dispatch copies," the lady replied.

'Yippee,' I'm thinking. Lyle had painted the picture beautifully. Had I not seen lightning splinter a tree before, I might have been babbling by now. Four long pine "spears" had shot away from the tree trunk, traveling forty feet or so before jamming cleanly into the earth. Each spear was burning, like a western movie gone crazy. Most interestingly, the spears stuck in evenly spaced intervals from their neighbors and at precisely the same angle from the snag. Mother's precision, even now.

It was many miles to the nearest pond, so once Lyle took a thorough look at the snag and determined that the fire hadn't burned deep into the heart, he had me shut down the ship and directed the crew to take action. I had been hoping for a call to deploy the trusty water bucket, but there was no urgency, and I reminded myself about my predecessor's admonition: "Let the Indians run the show!"

Still, any good chopper driver with water-bucket experience is like a wired greyhound behind the starting gate when the smell of smoke is in the air!

Lyle knew the no-water-drill: Dirt, shovels, and Pulaskis. The crew got busy putting a fire line around the snag, pulling out the burning spears and tossing them inside the fire line (reverently) and flinging shovel after shovel of good ol' Mother Earth upon the flames.

Many shovels-full later, one of our two backpacks of precious water was offloaded from the ship's basket and applied judiciously to the most stubborn coals. Tiny streams of water were sprayed with patience, and they finished the job. After the little water-bladder was exhausted, Lyle directed the time-honored final step: Shaving off the burnt surface wood with sharp Pulaski blades, feeling with the hand for deeper heat, possibly hiding within the snag.

Satisfied at last that the fire was out, Lyle checked the sun against his wristwatch and made the call:

"Dispatch, the Snag Fire is under control. Recommend Black Rock keep an eye out for a few days. 66 Foxtrot will be airborne momentarily, returning to base."

And so it went, smoky flight suits, char on our faces, rifles rolled up in blankets for the brief flight down to Window Rock. Easy money.

With the start sequence hanging on Lyle's command, I sat poised with my left hand around the throttle grip and my right index finger on the start button.

I couldn't help but notice how Lyle seemed a little taller, maybe a trace more swagger to that thoroughbred stride of his as he swung himself up into the right front seat of our dandy little flying machine.

And there was that grin again. Looking right at me he barked, "Home, Cowboy!" And to a man we damned near fell out of our seats laughing.

Ship Rock: Tse Bit a i – the Winged Rock

Author's Note: *Many thanks to my old friend, playwright, and story teller Dennis Freeman for his collaboration in this story. Dennis also flew in Vietnam. We've both found the Navajo Nation to be a retreat from where we've been and a destination for our wandering feet.*

HELICOPTER LIGHTNING!

A Shocking-But-True Tale From Central Nevada

Whenever I experience a particularly interesting event in my trade, I faithfully manage to find time to share it with my old friend and mentor, Peter H. Gillies. Pete and I are commercial helicopter pilots, and if there is anything we have in common beside our gray hair, it is our mutual love of piloting rotorcraft, especially in remote locations.

I recently returned from one of those special jobs, took out a raggedy writing tablet and pencil, and wrote from Boise, Idaho:

> "Dear Pete,
> The concrete pouring job in central Nevada is now in the books, and according to four of the construction men at the top of the mountain, the 'helicopter lightning' was intense!
> The job required a Bell Super 204B helicopter to sling thirty-odd yards of the heavy gray mud to the summit of Mt. Callaghan, some 10,200 feet of snow-capped splendor overlooking endless miles of prime, high Nevada ranchland in every direction.
> Contributing to the pour was a Bell LongRanger, which carried one-quarter yard of concrete every six minutes from the mixing site at the end of the road to the summit. We had to employ two ships to keep the mixture from aging before all thirty yards were delivered to the deep forms the crew had excavated into the crown of the peak.

The LongRanger was piloted by John Kelly, a talented veteran with a handlebar moustache…usually the sign of a former Cav pilot!

Both helicopters were using one hundred-foot long-lines made of braided wire rope, terminated by your standard lightweight aluminum concrete bucket.

As the afternoon progressed, John and I began to speculate over our air-to-air radio about the darkening clouds gathering upwind from our range of mountains. A little shower wasn't our concern, but the clouds spelled favorable conditions for…you guessed it: static electricity.

And, as we both know, the Huey's forty-eight-foot main rotor churning overhead turns into a heck of a generator under these conditions. From the rotor system it can instantly zip through the mast and down the steel line to the three-quarter yard concrete bucket. Lots of hot little protons looking for an electrical ground.

John radioed the ground crew to get out their rubber gloves and static-discharge tools, and upward we lumbered.

Moments later, as I powered the old bird up through 9,000 feet, I detected a small but surly little cloud, inching closer and closer to a point above the peak - where I would soon be hovering over the crew. Raindrops began to peck at the bubble window as I called upon the old gal's thirteen hundred ponies to levitate the bucket toward the pit.

The first man in line at the pit held out a long, wooden-handled shovel with a heavy wire fastened to the metal blade, a fine makeshift grounding wand. He firmly planted the blade against the bucket's metal frame as it floated by, and much to my amazement, brilliant flashes of electrical current burst out at the point of contact, as bright as any arc-welder!

The arcing continued for over five seconds, at which time the worker separated himself from the tool and sprinted away.

This startling activity was hidden from the two other men standing on the pit's scaffolding, who eagerly reached for the bucket's dangling tag lines. The next in line was greeted with a four-foot long bolt of high-amp inspiration, which streaked from the tag line to his fingertips, sending him reeling to the ground. Fetal position.

Before I could pull away, the last man in line—now quite aware that this was one Concrete Bucket From Hell - leaped heroically from the scaffolding toward salvation, only to catch a bolt in the posterior when he landed.

My helmet's earphones popped loudly as each bolt shot from the bucket, and the scene below was punctuated by three grown men—spread out on the ground—doing their own versions of the Funky Chicken!

The fourth hombre, whose job it was to give hand signals, had yet to taste the wrath of my nasty bucket, but he was giving me a signal which clearly indicated his disinterest.

Down the mountain I clattered with my ton of electrically charged concrete, much to the relief of the ground crew. However, within fifteen minutes, the cloud was gone, the men had recovered their composure, and the pour continued, although with an air of anticipation.

Hours later, the pour was capped and wrapped – as they say – and I raced a thunderhead on a parallel path back toward our tent village near a dude ranch.

Pulling maximum cruise power, I whipped out a crop duster turn just west of our tent village and got the skids on the ground, no more than twenty seconds before the thunderstorm hit the camp. I rode it out with the rotors at flight idle, watching to my left as one tent after another yielded to the fifty knot winds and slashing rain. No lightning this time, but everyone's gear got soaked!

That evening, we gathered around the camp fire and, over some well-deserved cold beer, the hands delighted the rest of us with their versions of 'helicopter lightning,' That job is done, and *man*—it was one to remember.

Your buddy,
Wingo"

Helicopter Lightning!

FLYING THE DYNAFLIGHT-SEISBAG

Three Dimensional GPS and the Bag-Runner in Action

"The stars at night are big and bright, (clap-clap-clap-clap)
Deep in the heart of Texas,

The sage's bloom is like perfume, (clap-clap-clap-clap)
Deep in the heart of Texas!"

A great ol' song if you're from Texas, and I used-to-was. And I seen all them stars on the long, early mornin' drive out to the helicopter, way southeast of Midland. This is mythical endless Texas mesquite ranch country, interrupted by cougar, cattle, huge rattlers, and horsy-style rockin' oil pumps. Cowboy yodelin' country.

The pilot I was relieving had been at it for forty days and nights, and it showed. He stood there with the JetRanger's key in his hand, and a far-away look in his eye. He was ready to go home, and the sun wasn't even castin' a shadow yet. But I was glad "Willy" was there to hold my hand while I tried out a couple of new contraptions, the DynaNav and the Bag-Runner.

I cut my long-line teeth during the "Seismic Boom" of the Seventies, and it was such good flying that I spent all my money on cameras and film just trying to capture it. Up in God's Country, buried in the snow. (Long hair, sunglasses, scraggly beard, big smile, you might have flown with me.)

"Old Seismic" was two-dimensional. "New Seismic" is a lot more high tech now-a-days. The seismic company's product is a 3-D trace, a computerized reflection, revealing the Earth's deeper secrets like never before. Valuable information in this day and age.

So when an old friend-slash-chief-pilot recently called me at home and said "seismic," I jumped about forty feet in the air, and almost offered to do it for free. Then Lourdes reminded me that I'd be leaving her and the kids again and that I owe; so I got back on the phone and demanded top dollar...and got something in between. (Man, did I fool him.)

Anyhow, Willy couldn't head for the airport until I showed the customer (about forty of them, actually) that I could repeatedly: A) Navigate to any particular point among the 1100 precise points on the fifty-square-mile project; B) Lay out a two-hundred pound seismic equipment "bag" at a chosen point, and; C) Go back later and pick up all them bags again, using a new-fangled device that requires no human contact. "Automatic." It says so right there on the thing! Automatic? Well, not at first.

How hard could it be, I had to ask, because I'm an old seismic hand, right? Well, first of all, I've been Huey-loggin' from the left seat for almost ten years, with a customized bubble door, armrest, drink holder, HBO and AOL. Now all I gotta do is lean way out the open door of this little ol' chopper and fly it from the right seat, no big deal. Seems easy enough. [Is that there the starter button?]

I never felt so rusty in my whole life! The right door sent me back to the novice ranks in skill level until...an hour or so later, I talked myself into "just doing it," and then I spent the next two weeks knowing the precise location of one particular muscle in my lower left hip area that enables a person to hang out the right door all day long. That out-of-shape muscle paid me back, night and day, with an ache that had to approximate childbirth. We're talkin' warp sniveling, here! [I must be gettin' old.]

The DynaFlight-SeisBag (a name only its mother could love) is a fairly new device patented by DynaNav Systems, Inc. that incorporates a GPS/GLONASS DynaByte processor unit and projects navigational data onto a compact TV screen [Dyna-Viz] hung just to the right of the 206's instrument panel. Accuracy to one meter or better, says the manufacturer.

The processor unit sits opposite the pilot in the left forward nose area. A box about the size of a toaster oven, the DynaByte processor uses a flashcard adapter and a data card to update the points where bags are to be "deployed" or "retrieved." The customer downloads the targets onto the flash card and provides that card to the pilot at the start of a mission.

So what you do is, plug the flash card into the "brain," and light off the Allison. While things are spooling up, the display comes on line. Once the program is booted up, the pilot uses the "Grip Switches" on the "Button Pad" (mounted on the collective, in this bird) to scroll through several lines and stations, and "enters" the station number where the bag is to be deployed. Now you go where the satellites point you.

From where I first lifted off, the DynaViz arrow indicated: fly southeast for 6.3 kilometers. Yep, everything is metric. Off I flutter, levitating four two-hundred pound bags on a four-hook carrousel at the end of my one hundred-foot long-line. I'm used to a one hundred-eighty-foot line, so it took a while to get my regular flying speed up.

As I zipped along at the ragged edge of VNE with one door off, grinning from ear to ear…the DynaViz counted down the distance backwards. Within 1.5 clicks, the screen began to trickle down little golden plus signs, giving me a crude rate of closure, as it jumped down from 800m, 600m, etc.

The last fifty meters are done slowly, as the arrow becomes a three-dimensional flagpole on the screen. A twirling "X" appears at its top if you're within a few meters of dead center, and—if you're not dragging all four fabric bags through the sharp thorns and cacti by then— you're doing pretty good! (I wonder if we can't move the DynaViz screen into the doorway, more along my line of sight?)

Once you get the "X" centered within the smallest box, you are precisely where the satellites want you. Now you simply flip that tiny switch on the Button Pad to the (down) "deploy" position, which (A) Releases the bag, and (B) Records "station number so-and-so deployed." That's correct, it tells on you. *Does it ever!*

So "deploying" is pretty straight forward, but there are 'slips between the cup and the lip,' as the good Bard is wont to remind us. Some bags' contents are "special," and they can't be dropped off at just any old station. The carrousel's upward-shining red light signifies that the "special" hook is next in sequence, so you control your own fate.

Other things go wrong, believe me; and you'll be expected to land and correct what's wrong in some pretty thorny situations. Or admit defeat and call in a Trouble Shooter, who has a long drive on a "Quad" to try and undo the problem, i.e., a "special" bag dropped off at the wrong point.

"Retrieving" bags employs the Bag-Runner, patented by Rupert's Land Operations, up in Canada. Switching them out, you'll hold a one hundred-foot hover while the staging manager disconnects the four-hook carrousel unit and reconnects the same longline and electrical cord to the Bag-Runner, and you're off like a Prom dress.

Simply put, you navigate to the first retrieval point (using the DynaNav, of course) and when you get there, lower the bag runner over a nubbin stuck in the top of a plastic cone. The Bag-Runner latches on to the nubbin, while you remember to move that tiny little switch upward this time to inform the computer that you've "retrieved" the bag, and haul away.

The nubbin is connected to a nylon rope, which threads through the cone and cinches up the bag. You could theoretically pick up six or seven nubbins in all, if the bags were light enough.

That's the fun part! But, there are so many things that can go wrong flying the Bag-Runner that I shrink from the chore of trying to document them.

It has more to do with the terrain, the vegetation, the way the cones are laid out…and the weather, than it has to do with the Bag-Runner. It's pretty slick.

Once you get good at it and learn how to stay out of trouble (like knocking the nubbin off the cone; or moving the switch the wrong direction and "deploying" a bag right where you just "retrieved" one (now what?!) This is about as much fun as you can have with a JetRanger strapped to your back. *And* you get paid to do it. Now go pack that bag!

Returning to Mother...

Recollections of Three Close Calls

All helicopter pilots are trained from the git-go to keep an eye peeled for a place to put 'er down in the event the engine loses power. Fortunately, for our sake and the industry at large, this rarely happens. Nonetheless, we've been programmed to keep at least five hundred feet between us and Mother Earth—whenever possible—and to keep those eagle eyes a'roamin'.

(Remember the advice from a wise old pilot before our time: There's nothin' more useless than the altitude above you, the runway behind you, or the gas you left behind?) So we are forced to ponder the fact that Mother is always tugging on us, and only the power coming from that banging-metal engine or gas turbine can keep us up where the air is cool and the bugs are few.

Every now and then, however, we get an opportunity to display just how vigilant we have been and how much heed we've been paying to the old sages who signed off our tickets. In my case, I made it through the Army's flight training program (WORWAC) with nary a sneeze from any of the Hiller OH-23s' Franklins or Bell TH-13s' and UH-1s' Lycomings, all the way to Vietnam. It was there I got my first taste of reality, and it was a kinder and gentler wake-up call, at least for Memorable Event Number One.

It was March, 1969: I had been flying in the right seat of a "D" model Huey as a "peter pilot" for less than one month under the guiding hand of WO1 Dennis Foracker, getting a thorough orientation around II Corps near Pleiku. Activity had been light since my arrival and I was actually beginning to relax, enjoying my patriotic adventure.

Our first mission that day was to pick up a Lieutenant Colonel and a few grunts at LZ Oasis and drop them off at our 4th Division airstrip at Camp Enari. These lucky soldiers had finished their tours and were goin' home. It was plain to see by their joyous faces that they were loving their last chopper ride on their return trip to The World. Dennis had me shoot the approach to the base of the Camp Enari Tower, while I tried to relax him with smooth control movements. Mr. Foraker had seen some bloody hell near Ban Me Thout recently—he was not what I'd call a happy camper.

All was groovy until the last ten feet of the approach to the perforated steel deck, when a shrill high frequency noise and vibration came over the ship. It gently lost power and slid a few feet to a halt. I called out over the intercom, "I've got a noise and vibration!" Dennis also noted the high EGT reading and took over, shutting the aircraft down on the spot.

The troops were out of the ship and running before I got out another word, looking over their shoulders with eyes wide open as they double-timed toward the nearest shade. We had all really lucked out, and it wasn't lost on them. The problem? Foreign object damage (FOD) to the compressor. No big deal. A new engine was installed in under three hours and the Huey was back in the air for night missions.

Memorable Event Number Two would be my shortest flight ever: Several months later, same airstrip, different Huey. Our bird was parked in between two five-foot tall walls of steel planking and sandbags (a "PSP revetment," in military jargon) which provided a degree of protection from mortar and rocket attacks when the ship was parked. I had made Aircraft Commander by then and was assigned to a choice little operation that even now I can't elaborate upon, but we were known around the area as the "Elephant Branders."

The aircraft was another "D model" and was loaded to the gills with JP-4 and a bunch of other stuff that brought us up to max gross takeoff weight. My peter pilot that day was a newly promoted first lieutenant we addressed as "Flaming Dork"—when he wasn't around. In the back were two enlisted soldiers who did stuff you don't want to know about, neither. I felt generous that morning and had the good lieutenant take the controls and lift the ship out of the revetment, which I recall was his first "solo" attempt at the task. I was a little apprehensive but trying my best to act nonchalant, since the revetment allowed only about two feet of breathing-room on either side of the Huey's horizontal stabilizers.

The good lieutenant was a bit of a nervous stick—in my humble opinion, anyway. (To be fair, all us Elephant Branders felt pretty cool when we could gracefully slide our "H model" out of the worst revetment in the Division, by merit of the excessive degree of slope at our end of the strip.)

Flaming Dork had it all wound up as I radioed the tower "Blackjack 491, lifting from the south east revetments." My peter pilot announced over the intercom "Coming up!"

I was trying hard to not to touch the controls as the nose rose slowly, wandering slightly to the right, then to the left as he milked the right skid, then the left skid-heel off the ground and suddenly BOOOOMMM!!

The ship's nose swung quickly left and there we were, cross-wise above the revetment walls and I'm thinkin' the lieutenant had hit the wall on the way up!

I quickly got on the controls and called out "I've got it," while applying right cyclic, doing some serious shuckin' and jivin' with my feet while milking the energy out of the rotor system. The ship's caution panel was lit up big time and our chunky main rotors above us were slowing down, as the Huey settled gently back down to Mother…(or Mama-san, in this case) without lowering the pitch!

(What the…!??)

Flaming Dork and I were on the same wavelength by then, realizing something had let go and we were right back where we started—a flight lasting maybe four or five seconds!

I was busy radioing the tower that we'd had "some kinda mishap" and turning off switches before noticing that I was the only occupant of the aircraft.

My crew, followed by Flaming Dork, had headed for the concertina wire a hundred feet to my twelve o'clock. I was left to slide my armored seat's chicken-plate aft alone, a job relegated to the left side guy-in-back. In their haste, they had left me sittin' pretty, all alone.

In seconds, the crash trucks arrived and I began hearing apologies from my guys about leaving me behind. The maintenance chief showed up, and—without saying a word—unlatched the right-side engine cowling; reached in with his right hand, and scooped up a whitish looking, hot dusty pile of material just under the big Lycoming's bleed-band.

"Here's your engine, Chief!" he said, letting the stuff pour slowly from his hand like a Navajo sand painter.

Sure enough, we'd ingested a Dzus fastener on lift off, taking the second compressor row and everything aft clean down to the bone—and turned it all into powder. Several of our fellow Blackjack buddies had witnessed the shortest flight of our careers, and they colorfully described the event with its huge blow-torch flame shooting several feet past the tail rotor as we gyrated over the revetment. (No Broken Wing Award, though. Rats!)

With your indulgence, gentle readers, I'd like to squeeze in one more, since we're having so much fun. Let's shift to Corona, California, June 6th, 1991: Let me remind you that at the beginning we were addressing the importance of keeping a landing site in mind as we flutter along above Mother Earth on our magic carpet.

Harvey Brown, a man twenty years my senior, arrived at Hiser Helicopters' base early in the morning to be flown to his job site about thirty minutes south of town. Harvey was the V.P. of an electrical contracting company and was enjoying a cigarette as he described the power-line task ahead of us. Make that two cigarettes.

Wire pulling was the mission that day, one of my favorite assignments, and Floyd Hiser's Hughes 500 "D" had the left front pilot's door removed, topped off with Jet-A, and ready to rock. We saddled up for what sounded like a two-hour flight: pulling sock-line through a few miles of wood-pole structures.

Corona Airport sits about a half-mile north of one the busiest freeways in the world. The infamous 91 Freeway runs from Riverside through Orange County, eight lanes of bumper-to-bumper traffic this time of the morning. I mention this because our normally trusty little helicopter only took us about a half-mile.

Right after we left the pattern and leveled off at four hundred feet (under a partial overcast) Harvey began telling me about his exploits in Alaska when he was in a Bell 212 accident. I headed south, coming up on the 91 Freeway. (Everybody all together now:) BOOM!

Yep, there she went, a big yaw to the left and all I can see coming up below us are lots and lots of cars. The panel is lit up like the proverbial Christmas tree, whistles and bells, dirt and maps flying around. Harvey has grabbed the hand loop on the door and ceased his monologue. "We're goin' down!" I announced to my white-knuckled passenger.

Shoving the collective pitch down, I throttled back and trimmed the cyclic forces aft to a 60-knot attitude, wondering if the far-side freeway shoulder was wide enough to accommodate us or not.

I resisted the impulse to pry my eyes away from the scene ahead to steal a peek at the rotor tach, gauging instead by ear that we've got low-green rpm at best. Oh good, looking past the shoulder of the freeway, I see a small triangular grassy field surrounded by <u>wires!</u>

Not good!

Check that. The wires come out of the adjacent electrical sub-station and are beyond my proposed touchdown point, but as we came sailing on down to Momma, there was a barbed-wire fence to clear on short-final!

Suddenly I realized the engine is still running. Huh?! I decide to do a throttle-up and a little pitch-pull before we get to the fence and see if there's any power available, in case I end up short.

The rotor RPM quickly dropped further toward the low end and I'm back at flat pitch and cursing at myself for experimenting with a wounded engine. Now the flare, just enough to keep the tail feathers out of the barbed wire, level the tip path and plunk, bounce, skid... skid...skid.

We slid for about twenty feet, while the rotors swished slowly by around us, but we're down safe with no further damage. Whew!

The turbine was still running—for some strange reason! I elected to leave it running (for the customary cool-down? I asked myself later). I jumped out to open the engine clam-shell doors and take a look. My feet were the second pair to hit the ground, because Harvey had already bailed and was lighting up his third cigarette, before I got the clam-shell doors open.

Once the engine was exposed, I noticed that familiar powder clinging in abundance to the interior of the Allison 250-C20B engine housing. I remembered the choice words from the NCO back in 'Nam, "There's your engine."

I sensed a new commotion around us and looked around to see several of "Corona's Finest" police and fire vehicles streaming through the gate by the sub-station, Code Three! Probably a hundred eyewitnesses along the 91 Freeway—equipped with cell-phones, had dialed "911" as we went smokin' by.

Some time later, Floyd Hiser drove up and shook my hand, clearly grateful that all he'd lost was an engine. Harvey was gone by then, picked up by my buddy, Pete Gillies—in another 500D, to get that sock-line job finished.

A flat-bed wrecker that was summoned to retrieve the ship, arrived an hour or so later. Ironically, while exiting through the gates of the sub-station, the wrecker driver turned too sharply to the right and bent the crap out of the tail rotor. Ouch!

Once the 500 was back at Hiser Aviation, the compressor case was split open. The cause of the engine failure was obvious: the plastic liner around the compressor was eroded, allowing the liner to come into contact with the compressor blades, bending them instantly into a tangled mess.

So, my friends, if there's anything to be gleaned from these little gems of years gone by, I guess it would be that no matter what mission might have propelled you into the sky, I feel obligated to reiterate: It's never too early to start looking for a place to land, 'cause Mother is always pullin' on you!

CWO Wingo in Konthum, Vietnam - II Corps, with Blackjack Six. Wingo painted this and several other noses for Alpha Company.

Miss America Visits the 'Nam

Here she comes, ready or not!

One day back in good ol' 1969, Miss America made her rounds of South Vietnam. Wherever she traveled, young pilots like myself were taken off combat assault rolls and ordered to fly her and her entourage around in the newest Huey we had available. That meant that the "H" model had to be all spit-shined and gleaming. And that meant that the pilots had to help make it that way, because there was a lot to do and only four people to do it, practically overnight.

I recall having mixed emotions about flying the mission. On one hand, I feared the rush of distracting hormones that most of us manly types suffered from upon being suddenly exposed to a helicopter full of gorgeous, radiant women. On the other hand, I was embarrassed to be assigned a non-combat job.

Being one of the newer peter pilots at Camp Enari, home to the "Famous Fighting 4th" Infantry Division, I was at the beck and call of my Company Commander. If Major Griffiths wanted Wingo to fly the right seat of the "V.I.P." Huey, then by gosh, Wingo was available. There were worse jobs.

So there I was and here they came, an hour or so late. I tried not to look at the beauties; just did my duties, setting up the ship to crank as the XO showed the lovely ladies into their seats and seat belts—taking a lot longer than I thought was necessary. The young Captain probably fell into a daze back there amongst the cluster of fragrant All-American belles dressed in camouflage—yet looking good enough to eat.

I tried to keep my thoughts on the turbine engine's N1 and exhaust gas temp amid their charming, melodious giggles; roasting an engine at this point would not get me any Brownie points.

The fire base we were flying to was about half an hour west of Camp Enari, and I can't begin to remember its name, as they came and went under the direction of Major General Pepke. If the CO at the firebase knew of Miss America's approach, I don't think he bothered informing a certain combat infantryman who chose that time of the morning to head for the head. And who on Earth put the incredibly dusty helicopter LZ next to the head? Whomever, the guy had a military sense of humor.

Now that I think about it, it probably was a secret to the average infantryman that some of the finest-looking, unattached American women alive were only a minute away. No sense in telling Charlie about our precious cargo, as he was not above ruining our day at any given moment.

No one could have been less aware of Miss America than the brave, temporarily clean and shirtless GI who faced the morning sun and calmly dropped his shorts. He bowed, taking a seat on the open-air slit trench's wooden stoop as our slick banked in his direction. My final approach over the fire base's wire-strewn perimeter was deliberately hot, zeroing-in on a red smoke grenade just upwind of the head. Such a maneuver was well within what we aviators called a standard tactical approach.

The Huey was heavy with fuel and the Highland's density altitude was over six thousand feet that day, as usual. Picking my spot, the skids slid onto the ground with forward momentum near the smoke canister, as I reduced collective pitch. I kept one eye on the smoke, and the other on our disbelieving GI, seated thirty feet away—his olive drab skivvies down around his ankles. I heard the XO key his foot mike as he looked forward for the first time and took in the scene unfolding at twelve o'clock.

"HOLY SH _ _!" the Captain gushed, as the ugliest cloud of dust in all of II Corps boiled under the Huey's forty-eight-foot main rotor and raged in the direction of those green skivvies. At the last second, the GI looked up with an expression of…not again! Resigned to his fate, he leaned forward, turned his head to the side, and clenched his eyes tightly shut. His precious roll of paper began to spin and flutter, as he tightly gripped the rough wood board behind his bent knees with both hands. The nasty red dirt momentarily obscured his image, tearing at him like an angry herd of tumbleweeds.

You could hear the lovely ladies gasp in unison behind us as the hapless soldier went feet up and over backwards, the roll of toilet paper shot skyward, unraveling. It was a scene burned forever into the windshield—never to be forgotten by manly warriors, nor virginal beauty queens.

As the dust cleared, our vista became the backlit underside of the wooden bench: Several uniformly sawed privy holes were all lit up horizontally, left to right. Toilet paper waved gaily from yonder perimeter's concertina wire. Behind hole number three, the naked GI reclined on his backside in the warm, red dirt. Slowly, his right arm rose, and he flipped Miss America the bird, through hole number two.

Rat Wars!

Helicopters, horseplay, and hanta virus?

Working on the North Rim of the Grand Canyon a couple of decades ago, my young expectant wife and I were camped out—snug as a bug—in an old Airstream trailer. "Valentino" was nestled in a cozy spot under several large Ponderosa pines, away from the droves of tourists that came to see the higher up and most beautiful side of the Canyon. Built in 1960, our twenty-eight-foot twin-axle Land Yacht had seen better days, but for a workin' man's rig, it was hard to beat. A gorgeous Alpaca hide—here and there—made for frequent snuggling. Hence the bambino, I suspect.

Just a half-mile from the campground was our construction yard and the helicopter's NPS-approved Landing Zone. Rocky Mountain Helicopters' SA-315B Lama was the customer's aerial taxi and light crane for our long-term contract in the bottom of the Canyon, just around the corner from Bright Angel Falls.

The LZ was about a hundred feet from the same staggering abyss the diners in the Grand Lodge Dining Room basked at thru all them huge windows. The yawning abyss beckons over a fine, fruity, room temperature Cabernet Sauvignon, while hundreds of tourists savor medium rare Chateau Briand or Rock Lobster Almondine served by white-coat waiters.

After flying the crew of twelve down into the abyss every morning, I would sometimes get a short break. That's why I had my 250cc Yamaha "Enduro" motorcycle parked next to the LZ: To zip back to the Airstream and peel a juicy red mango for my pretty woman, or something.

The customer assigned me a portable radio so the foreman could reach me if they needed anything down below. Jumping on the bike, I could breeze back and forth down the old Jeep trail from our secluded corner of the woods. If the call for an aerial delivery of some sort came in, I'd be back in the saddle and flying in five minutes. This was one of those spectacular, adrenaline-rush fun jobs, with a short commute to boot.

Then the weather cooled down and here came the danged rodents! We discovered literally overnight that the rodents knew all the ropes about getting into an old trailer. That first chilly night was plenty scary for my little Mexicana; mice skittered here and there, over the blankets, squeaking and chewing—despite a heavy barrage of flying paperback novels and Kaibab moccasins!

Turning on a flashlight was a really bad idea, 'cause Lourdes got a good look at the herd. It was impressive even to me—an Okie-fied, battle-hardened chopper pilot—seein' all them beady little eyes glowing back at us from all corners of our little love nest. I gotta confess, it gave me the creeps!

I wasted no time the next morning searching for their entrances and rounding up a couple of mousetraps. Baiting them with peanut butter, the traps started snapping long before bedtime. I displayed my first mangled trophy to my snuggle bunny; her nose barely visible – peeking from under the thick quilts that Momma made. "Eee-youu!" came her muffled response; she disappeared back under the covers.

I dropped the dead units just outside the door—and reloaded the traps. By midnight, there was a sinister pile of fuzzy varmints by the front step, a pile which continued to grow until breakfast. "We'll need more traps," I reminded Lourdes, who mumbled something back at me in Spanish. Not a good sign.

Thirteen varmints the first night, and seventy-two by the end of the week. (I kept score using hash-marks on the back of the broom-closet door.) The mice herd began to slack off a bit after that, and we both started getting some sleep. I have to admit, though—a creative personality has a hard time ignoring such a fine catch of pelts, ripening outside his door every morning. T'was a shame to shovel 'em into the trashcan when they looked so cute with their tails trapped under the windshield wipers of my prankster work buddies.

My comrades' pickups were parked idling each workday morning outside the trailer; warming-up their defrosters for the short drive to the LZ, where they'd load the Lama's external baskets with their tools and grub. My thoughtful gift of animated dead rodents was the Okie way of sharing the bountiful harvest.

When the Canyon Boys eventually loaded up and engaged their truck's wipers to clear off the heavy morning dew—Haw! "Very funny, Wingo!" I heard Steve Mankle whine, as the little critters made grim mousey-arches on their rig's dirt-streaked windshields.

"Ha—-ha—-ha." And off they dieseled.

The next day I took Lourdes for a gentle little motorcycle ride through the Ponderosas along the North Rim, during a work break. Upon my return to the helicopter, I killed the bike's ignition and started to walk off. Immediately I heard the sound of bacon frying, and smelled a sharp, unfamiliar odor. Curious, sniffing the air cautiously… my Okie nose and ears zeroed in on the source.

The smoke and sizzle was coming from the top of my Yamaha's hot cylinder head! My Canyon Pals had returned the favor. Two partially fried gray mice were sizzling in between the cooling fins around the spark plug cap: Rodentia al dente. And me with no salsa!

After that little trick, I began to lay off the dead-mousey pranks, 'cause they were starting to give me the creeps. (Wasn't the Black Plague spread by the fleas of rats?!)

A day or two went by cautiously and I soon deduced that all was forgiven and forgotten.

Then I got a radio call, asking me real nice to fly on down to the new NPS Guest House we had just finished building along the Bright Angel trail. They were giving a tour of the spacious new redwood structure, which had a couple of them new-fangled electric toilets!

Mankle and the boys were standing there to greet me, real courteous and all. "Merkel" signaled me to shut 'er down and come on in for a look. I did just that, parked on the new prefabbed sectional concrete heliport, which a Bell 214 and my little Lama had recently built. It was a beauty, and large enough for a Huey to stretch out on.

The boys showed me inside the redwood lodge and all around, making sure I got to see the toilets in action and the fine easterly view through large windows, framing the sexy French helicopter as she sat there on the helipad. A photo op! But soon the tour was over, and I was sent off with a canister of blueprints, which were allegedly to be flown up for some NPS engineers to play with.

Climbing back into my sunny plastic cabin, I noticed that all the guys were lined up on the redwood porch, watching me admiringly as I began doing pilot things. Milking it for all it was worth, I got all harnessed in and made faces as the noisy Artouste IIIB turbine engine howled thru its automated start—whereupon I revved her up to clutch engagement speed. Rotors engaged, I reached up for my flight helmet.

My lightweight helmet hung from the twin, overhead hooks. Grabbing it ceremoniously with both gloved hands, I casually flipped it over backwards onto my head. Plunk, flop!! Something hideous bounced off my head, raked past my shades and into my lap.

It was a big, cold, brown, dead rat—with his mouth wide open and his black tongue hanging out. The Boys were having themselves quite a laugh, on yonder porch.

Pretty funny, indeed!—Awww rrrrats!—Another short break was in order, up top. Following a quick flight up to the Rim, an inordinately brisk bike ride to Vermintino, I threw open the little aluminum door and exclaimed, "Amor, I'm headed for the shower! And don't kiss me; I'll explain later!!"

Grand Canyon National Park—October, 1978.
Captain Methane gestures for friend and
photographer Dennis R. Freeman.

Never Fly With Your Brother in A Dive Bomber!

Chopper Pilot Meets Skyraider.

Camp Enari, II Corps—Vietnam. (Summer, 1969). The Orderly found me in my hooch, recovering from a night of too many Jack Daniels. My skull was painful to the touch, and "Purple Haze" was my situation. Last night's live Philippine Rock Band had outdone themselves. Erotic visions of the band's nymph-like Go-Go girls, gyrating in unison, those tiny bikinis…How did I wind up in my hooch, I wondered?

"Come on, Mr. Wingo, wake up!" The "Spec. 4" was pounding on my rickety rocket box door. "There's a Captain Wingo on the land line, Sir. You're wanted in Pleiku City, ASAP."

Bingo. That was the code my brother and I conjured up in the event he scored me a ride in one of his squadron's Skyraiders. "I'm comin'," I hollered back…no hangover was gonna' stand between me and no Skyraider ride!

Jon was assigned to the 366th Spad Drivers out of Pleiku Air Base, a scant six miles away from my 4th Inf. Div. chopper base. Dashing through the chow line with my Army flight helmet in tow, the world's worst Jeep driver got me to Pleiku in record time.

Soon I got the whole nine yards: Briefing, harness, parachute, survival gear, pistola, ("G Suit?? – They're for Sissies!!") and a thorough recheck of every little thing. Waddling out to the flight line like two big, fat ducks, I was beginning to appreciate the differences in which Jon and I went to war.

The Unit's A-1G model was the only two-holer around; we sat side by side as Jon showed me the ejection procedure, among other things. Before you could say "Shoot Howdy," we taxied out and were checking the mags at the north end of a ten thousand foot runway. Fifty-weight oil streaked the thick "bullet proof" windscreen as the sound of ten thousand Harleys bolted together split the air: Potato-Potato-Potato, etc.

The guy in the Pleiku Air Base tower announced "Clear for take-off" and the old tail dragger roared to life as Jon put the hammer down, the nose dropped, and Wobbly One Wingo was nailed to the right seat by the big ol' four bladed Hamilton Standard prop, now all a-blur. With nary a bullet in the racks, she was light—and before I knew it, we were way up in the cool air of the Central Highlands.

After proving to Jon that his chopper pilot brother knew nothing about acrobatic flying, we re-entered controlled flight and headed for LZ Penny, an abandoned Fire Base north of Pleiku. Several weeks prior, Jon's Spad unit had surprised a brassy NVA platoon as they marched straight across the huge circle of reddish brown dirt. Jon offered to show me how one FAC and two Spads turned an old Fire Base into a greasy spot.

The first roll-in was from around four thousand feet, at a fairly steep angle. The pullout measured four Gs on the meter in front of me, as Jon called out "Pickle Pickle Pickle!" over the crummy intercom. Back up into the blue we roared, going around for one more. [Absorbing the stress from the four-G pull-out, I thought to myself: Whew! This sure ain't no Huey ride!]

"And here's how we do it when we're receiving fire," Jon shouted over the screaming R3350 radial engine. Climbing rapidly to six thousand feet, LZ Penny momentarily looked more like LZ Microdot. I was suddenly fascinated by the altimeter: I'd never seen one unwind so fast! Looking through the oily windshield, the LZ quickly became humongous as Jon announced, "Pickle Pic-"

The worst had happened, the terrible roar of all those Harleys and a five hundred knot air stream convinced me. The Spad had shed her wings. I could actually see the headlines of the Las Cruces Sun News: "Brothers Die in Vietnam Crash!"

Slowly coming to, I heard laughter. I was doubled over, my Army helmet's microphone pointed toward my blood-engorged leather boots. It was Jon who was laughing, of course. The sight of his little brother laid out by 5.2 Gs was his reward for luring me into the cockpit. (So what if he had skipped the part about taking a deep breath—and holding it—as the pickles were passed out?)

In just a few minutes, I rewarded my thoughtful brother with a clear plastic baggy full of my quickly consumed Army mess hall breakfast, as I sat back and began to moan and sweat buckets. Jon flew us back to Pleiku like a little old granny lady.

In due time, the long runway finally came into view, and that was something to smile about. That, and knowing—some day soon—Captain Smarty Pants would learn the hard way:

Spad drivers can't hover!

Shoot-out at the Corner Bar!

Fearless and Me Get the Short End of the Stick!

'Long about nine o'clock in the mornin' me and "Fearless" Dougie Farfel pulled up to the dusty entrance at the front of the Corner Bar. The dust cloud we sucked along under our outfit's Ford pickup followed us on into the open door and billowed like thousands of tiny stars as we stood framed in the shaft of early morning light.

It was so dark inside it took awhile for our pupils to dilate and find our way around. Somebody hollered, "Howdy boys!" We hollered back and shuffled slowly toward the voice, feeling our way blindly along the barstools.

We were two tired chopper pilots, having just put our French helicopters to bed after a long night of flying "frost protection" missions over the L & D Ranch. That'd be where your Almond Joy & Mars bars get their almond crunch.

'Round about February through April, Mother Nature needed our help to keep the tender young almond flowers from freezing their little buds off. And our choppers usually did the job, blasting the warm air just above the trees down through the cold air, obliterating any chance of frost for up to an hour at a time. Once the sun rose, we became free men again until around dinnertime. Not bad for a couple of young, handsome bachelors on a spring job in central California!

Dougie & me was veterans from the 'Nam, so it was traditional to stop by the local watering hole on our way back to the hooch. We'd shoot the breeze and have a cold one while we unwound from hovering over the frosty almond orchards in the dark.

As I paid for the long necks, I heard Doug mumble something about a friendly little game of 8-Ball. He came up with a quarter, and about that fast, we was on our way to the back of the bar, where an old pool table stood quietly waiting for us.

We'd played at this table before, and she was a beauty. Regulation size, leather catch-pockets, level as the state of Texas, and nary a rip on its virginal green expanse. A big shaded lamp hanging low over the table sported Clydesdales haulin' the "King of Beers" through a picturesque Christmas scene. Merle Haggard was on the jukebox. Pool playin' just didn't get any better than this!

"Rack 'em, Easy Money!" I called out as Doug fingered his quarter.

The first game went down pretty slick, 'cept I lost and had to rack 'em as Dougie pulled out his fixin's and rolled a cigarette.

"Why don't you break down and buy a pack of smokes, Fearless?" I asked as he was putting the last of his spit down on the little ribbon of glue to finish the twirlin.' I already knew the answer:

"Cause I'd smoke 'em too fast if I did," he wheezed, firing up a big Ohio Blue Tip kitchen match off his bony backside, lighting up his cancer stick. He blew smoke all over the table (?) then meticulously placed the cue ball down near the center of the break circle and waited patiently, as I carefully pulled the wooden triangular rack off the colorful balls.

'Long about then I heard a commotion off to my left as the rear door of the bar swung open, brightening up the field of play for a second as an old man made his way over the threshold, limping. He hobbled along with the aid of a black wooden cane. A little over five foot tall and eighty years old if he was a day, we made eye contact briefly and his eyes gleamed like the sun off 'a chrome pistol!

I couldn't help but notice that he was holdin' a dollar bill in his left hand as he made his way between the pool table and my barstool. As I stood there with the rack in my hand, the old fellow slapped the dollar down on the rail next to me and announced profoundly to the three occupants of the building, "Dollar sez I sink the 8-ball on the break. Left side pocket!"

I looked at Doug. Doug looked at me. I smiled, straightened up, and started to offer the old fellow his dollar back, but then I noticed—in the big mirror on the wall—that the barkeep back yonder was grinning from ear to ear, noddin' his head like one'a them fuzzy bobble-head dogs in somebody's rear window.

"Done deal!" Doug and I said in the same breath, and I offered up my pool cue to the old gent. He ignored me and ambled around to the breaking end of the table, where he flamboyantly gestured for Fearless Dougie Farfel to stand aside. He then looked me straight in the eye and replied, "Don't need no stick, Sonny! I got my stick right here!"

And as comical as it looked, he raised that old crooked wooden cane up level with the table, showing Doug and me the standard old rubber-crutch tip at its dusty terminus.

Doug reminded me later that I snorted under my breath as the old geezer stepped up to the table, rared back and smacked that danged cue ball with a stroke as straight and true as Ralph Rudolf Wanderoni, Junior hisself. The sound was not unlike a fifty-caliber Hawkin rifle on a cold mornin'!

When the smoke cleared, as they say, the eight ball was rolling slowly along the last two inches of its journey, straight into the left side pocket, where it fell with a thud that I can still sometimes hear in my nightmares to this day.

Doug stood transfixed like some pitiful wax museum figure as I hesitantly peeled a new dollar out of my breast pocket and slid it under his. The old hustler collected his winnings and sauntered off toward the bar.

Looking up into the mirror, the bartender already had the man's cold beverage of choice waiting, and I knew that we'd been had. The look on the bartender's face was worth the dollar…the look on Dougie's face was priceless.

That was near thirty years ago, but if I ever do stop by Atwater again, the Corner Bar will be where I pull up. I gotta' find out how he did it. And how many notches the Corner Bar Hustler has on his cane.

You the Pilot?

Would you ever want to deny it?

I vividly recall, while enduring the Army's primary helicopter flight training, that to a man, we were so proud to be pilots. Well, not exactly yet, since we were still just a gaggle of lowly Warrant Officer Candidates and our silver wings were many months away, if ever.

Still, we had collectively given up our hair, our homes, and our freedom. Patriotically signing our lives away for the opportunity to become chopper pilots; wear those cool Ray-Bans and silky flight jackets and say "Roger" a lot.

We were pilots. And we wanted everyone to know it.

And then one morning this Military Science Instructor we so admired stoically informed us that pinning on those silver wings wouldn't make the slightest difference in our collective appeal to the opposite sex. We were floored! He was wrong. He had to be wrong. Adoring women were a must.

That was the first time I ever questioned if I really wanted to be a pilot. Up until then, being a pilot had meant everything to me. That was all that I dreamed of.

But I have met a pilot or two since then who, at least briefly in their flying careers, wished they weren't pilots. And "Captain Tom" comes to mind.

....

[Pop!!]

Tearing low-level across the rolling high country, Captain Tom made it look easy as his chopper's skids mowed down several old yucca stalks along the way. The old Hiller's turbocharged 540 Lycoming banging-metal engine roared through twin headers of hot blue steel, delivering what the Captain demanded with his size-eight left hand. Leveling the ship abruptly, a dry stalk jammed into the red position light fixture at seventy knots and stuck.

[Thonk!!]

Literally riding shotgun, "Jeffro," his right-seat door gunner yelled "Bulls eye" as the chopper's right skid toe fractured another pod not more than two feet from the business end of his Wingmaster. Without missing a beat, Jeff pulled the weapon up and fired from hip level, taking out the next dead vegetable in line.

[Ka-blam!!]

Captain Tom hooted his approval over his headset: "Ha-haaaa. Nothin' but chunks." Both men laughed as the Hiller dipped and darted toward the hogback ridge.

Having just done a one-eighty from an unsuccessful dog-hunt, the Captain had decided to have some fun along the way back, seeing as how they were out in the middle of nowhere. He and Jeffro had flown several "predator control" missions before, and as far as the two of them were concerned, low-level-over-the-coyotes was it!

Torqued up to red-line manifold pressure, the Captain traversed the incline cresting the razorback ridge, whereupon he shoved the cyclic forward—a daring 'negative g' maneuver that dumped the nose and yanked both men up against their lap belts; the spent double-ought 12-gauge cartridge floated skyward from the floor.

"Shoot howdy." Jeff howled, snatching the shell like a fly with his left hand. Suddenly the Captain banked hard left, the thirty-foot rotor blades popped loudly as he exclaimed "Ho-ly Mo-ly." Jeff pumped a fresh round into the chamber by reflex.

"Them ain't no coyotes, Jeffro, but look at all the stinkin' sheep!" To which Jeff had no response, for before he could say 'Que pasa, Calabasa,' Captain Tom dove down reeeeal low over the nucleus of the herd, yanking and banking and howling like Wolfman Jack! Hundreds upon hundreds of hysterical bleating sheep stampeded in every direction. The Captain was clearly on a roll.

Five minutes later, Jeff signed Tom's Operations Report as the Hiller ground-ran to cool off six red-hot cylinders, the shaking machinery making their jerky signatures look suspicious, if not half-drunk.

It was almost "Miller Time," or so it seemed.

Alfredo—the Hiller mechanic—was already busy pulling yucca top debris out of his skid's position light fixtures, muttering to himself about his joy-riding gringo pilot. He ambled off toward the limp 100 Octane fuel hose as the engine coughed to a stop and the rotor blades whistled slowly overhead.

"Thanks for yet another memorable ride, Tom." Jeff chuckled.

"See you tomorrow," Tom replied, pulling off his sweaty headset and stepping down from the cockpit. Jeff cleared the weapon's chamber, slipped the Wingmaster into its case, and headed for his Jeep.

Tom usually followed Jeff down the hill, but today, he had decided to install a new CB radio in his Ford 4X4. "The more gadgets, the merrier," he always said. He was soon inverted under the Ford's dashboard, a-drillin' and a-cussin'.

Done with refueling, Alfredo was now occupied wiping down the tail rotor drive shaft, getting the dirt out of the way for a thorough post-flight inspection. He was the first to notice the battered old 1950 Dodge pickup bouncing up the dusty road from beyond the distant hogback ridge. They weren't expecting anyone, especially anyone driving such an old beat-up piece of ...

Probably rubber-neckers, Alfredo rationalized, already wishing Tom would reappear to answer the inevitable litany of dumb questions that amateurs always seem to come up with. And here they came. Or was there just the driver?

Alfredo pushed his grimy bifocals back against his sweaty nose for a better focus. Then again, he mused, this guy didn't really look like the kind of man that stops to ask dumb questions. Stepping out of the little truck, he stood around six feet, but this one was "broad at the shoulder and narrow at the hip," as the song goes.

The mechanic started paying closer attention as the hombre bee-lined past Tom's rig and marched straight toward him. Alfredo could now see the man was sweating profusely, glaring, and grinding his teeth. His long dirty hair was tangled with broken twigs. He was coated with dust and festooned with bloody scratches. He looked Basque, somehow. Turns out, he did have one question:

"You the pilot?" he asked, his voice barely under control.

Alfredo's Army-conditioned brain ran through a few choice one-liners, normally reserved for wise guys—quickly rejecting every last one of them, as he recognized the intent in the angry man's eyes and the fragrance of a large sheep herd that followed his inquiry.

"That would be the Capitán," Alfredo offered in flawless Castillian Spanish, nodding toward Tom's Ford. Without another word, the sheepherder turned and stomped down the incline toward the pickup, clinching his fists and creating angry little dust clouds in his wake.

Tom was still upside-down, splicing the red wires together when he heard the heavy boots arrive at his open door, and the question barked from the stranger, "You the pilot?"

"That would be me, but I'm kinda' busy," Tom replied, just starting to tape over the bare hot-wire splice as the stranger grabbed both of his spotless size eight Adidas and hauled him rudely feet first out of the rig and onto the dirt.

Hollering "What the..." in protest, 12-volt fireworks erupted under the dash as the bare copper wires arced along behind him. Tom struggled to kick himself free from the stranger's iron-like grasp.

Once the pilot's backside was in the dirt, the sheepherder released his ankles and hauled him to eye-level by the front of his flight suit, getting up-close-and-personal with the smaller man.

"That was my herd you scattered from here to hell and back, pilot, and now I'm gonna kick your ass!"

And he did just that; a rather thorough ass-kicking it turned out to be, while Alfredo protested from a safe distance; and not in his loudest voice, as the story is retold.

After a few minutes, the Basque's big fists grew sore from pounding on the Captain's face, and he left, never to be seen again. As if anyone was going to go looking for him, after all the facts were known.

The Captain took some unscheduled time off after his butt-kicking. "A little R&R," according to Operations. Time to collect himself, re-evaluate his life's ambitions. Time for the swelling to go down. Finish wiring up that CB radio, maybe. Keep his line of work to himself, perhaps. Less low-level terrorizing and unabated howling, definitely! Burn that sheep-smellin' flight suit and start dressing like a logger, he reckoned.

An ironic twist came a couple of years later. Tom had moved on to a helicopter-logging outfit and was indeed dressing as a logger.....

One morning he was *sport loggin'* somewhere in the great northwest when his Huey's 42 degree gearbox let go. The Captain narrowly escaped serious injury in a nasty crash-landing into tall timber; the ship coming to rest inverted, near a fellow logger — one of his "hookers."

Emergency calls went out as two of the closest ground crewmen came running to rescue the Captain, who had fortunately only suffered a broken collarbone. After a few minutes to evaluate his condition and treat themselves for scrapes and cuts, all three hiked down the steep incline toward the log landing as the ambulance crew pulled up, Code Three.

Walking out through the tall brush, the first in line to reach the ambulance crew was the scratched-up hooker carrying Tom's flight helmet. Thinking the hooker was the pilot, the ambulance crew grabbed him and literally had to wrestle him down onto the clean sheets of the gurney, before the hooker could say "What the...!" At which time the Captain shouted above the confusion, "Hey, I'm the one who's hurt, I'm the pilot!" And I was glad to hear that you admitted it, Tom. (But where are the adoring women?!)

Pencil sketch of Lourdes based on her 1976 passport photo, which I whipped out during a three-month hitch away from the family.

Unique McPeak and the Classic Stall

A tad too much testosterone, times two.

Legend has it that an old (scarred) airplane flight instructor bore a tattoo on his behind, in bold font: "Don't Never, Ever Stall," something I'd be perfectly content to take his word for.

Truth is, I stalled my share of Cessnas getting ready for my ASEL Commercial flight check exam back in 1970. A decade would pass before I witnessed a Cessna stall on take-off, and – well, that gave the word a whole new meaning!

Rialto Municipal Airport (L67)—Jan '81: Western Helicopters' Bell 205A-1 sported a three-shades-of-mud paint scheme and she was rocking gently on the ramp in a steady 25-knot Santa Ana wind. Believe it or not, we were about to do a test flight for a high-wire stunt. A professional video cam sat running on a tripod, recording our trio: Western's Chief Pilot, Pete Gillies; stunt man slash high-wire artist, Steve McPeak; and this here Okie. Someone with McPeak's crew was making a documentary of our "intro" and the test flight.

"Unique" McPeak, as he was known in those days, was a daredevil of some fame. He had made high-wire history walking the breathtaking gondola cables high above Rio de Janiero. Even better, he spent days clinging to the steep, greasy cables—scrubbing them clean so he could "walk" them. In the end, he did it! His strong hands gripped a thirty-foot long balancing pole, with the Stars and Stripes at one end and the colorful flag of Brazil on the other. "No guts, no glory" was his motto. What a guy!

McPeak was also an unabashed self-promoter, and he was determined to be "the first to walk a high wire one mile high over the Hollywood Reservoir." Figured he'd hire a Huey to help him do it.

Once he got the idea in his head, there was no stopping him. McPeak spent several days expertly welding an "X" shaped, one-ton, steel truss contraption that coupled to hard points under the helicopter. Western's tarmac was the assembly area for his ambitious arc welding. Unique McPeak welded and welded, day after day—and well into the night. (Western's subsequent electrical bill was delivered by an eight hundred pound gorilla.)

McPeak's Hollywood plan went something like this: Once the helicopter attained a high hover, McPeak would climb out and (electrically) crank down a twenty-foot long, rigid steel pipe ("wire") which was deployed longitudinally below the helicopter. Once it was cranked down and locked, McPeak would make like a monkey, ease himself down to the "wire" and commence his high wire routine. For this first rehearsal flight, he had safety wires on either side to grab if he slipped—or something?

So there we were, ready to rock—and the durned windsock was stickin' straight out! A steady blast of air straight from the Cajon Pass threatened to never quit. McPeak was lookin' at the windsock and back at Pete. Back to the windsock—back at me.

I may have had my own reservations, but knowing Pete as I did, we were gonna give it a twirl—regardless. The steely-eyed son of a Grumman test pilot (and a WAF B-17 pilot), he naturally wanted to take the ship over the fence and wring it out, see how she flew with our Erector Set From Hell bolted to it—hurricane or no.

"The helicopter doesn't know the wind is blowing," Pete would always say.

With our wives, children, and girl friends looking pensive from the safety of their cars, we wrapped the interview and strapped into our respective seats. Director of Maintenance, Bill Dvorak, was standing by to unhook the 205's forty-eight-foot rotor for start-up, and man was I surprised to see a little Cessna 150 taxi out from Art Scholl Aviation's fuel island in the face of all that wind!

I commented to Pete over the intercom that it surely must be one of Art's "Air Show" buddies—they dropped by all the time in torpedo bombers, Gypsy Moths, Corsairs, Tri-Planes and Spit Fires – "Aces" mostly. Only this little airplane wasn't taxiing for runway three five, it was headed west down the taxiway for zero six! A crosswind takeoff in this wind? This guy must be good!

Somebody at the tail was hollerin' "Clear to crank!" while I sat harnessed to my uncomfortable mesh seat, watching as the little airplane commenced his roll—gaining speed, leaning left into the crosswind, when it suddenly rotated to his left—right in front of us.

The instant that aluminum bird lifted off the gusty runway, it pivoted left—into the wind—and hovered there: Rocking and bouncing in the rollicking Santa Ana Wind—pointed north—but going nowhere! And right as I was about to say, *Man, this guy is good,* the little airplane's tail dipped, the nose pointed to the heavens, and it climbed to about thirty feet AGL. And then the nose dropped sharply, and the airplane became a lawn dart.

"A classic stall," Pete narrated to our small group of spectators, as the Cessna shot straight into Mother Earth at full throttle. [Bbbrrrrrttt!]

"Call the fire department. Call the fire department." Pete shouted to no one in particular. He was five steps ahead of all of us, spearheading a speechless, wide-eyed group of rescuers toward a cloud of dust with a tail sticking out of it.

Closing in on the wreck, the next thing we saw was a bald-headed male struggle out of the busted right door of the Cessna, his headphones turned sideways on his bleeding head. Turns out, he was the pilot. He observed us running his way, and hollered, "My sister's hurt!" as he hobbled to the other side of the badly bent 150. A busted arm turned out to be the worst of it.

It was about an hour before the injured siblings were transported and we got the runway open again, returning (with blood stains and dirt here and there) to the site of our experimental high-wire act. Before we could persuade our wives and girlfriends that a little wind wasn't gonna stop us from flying, half of them threw up their hands, shook their heads and left! I can still hear McPeak hollerin' above the wind: "No guts, no glory!"

Turns out, McPeak's heli-high-wire rig worked pretty good. After Pete put the ship thru some maneuvers that scared the remaining observers half to death, he signed off on the stability factor. McPeak then cranked the device downward—and minutes later—walked up and down the tight wire that blustery afternoon – just a few feet off the ground.

After all was said and done, McPeak unloaded his toolbox and removed the complex rig. Said he was gonna make some modifications to it back in his garage. Hours later, he hauled his contraption off on a trailer and we never saw hide nor hair of him again.

A short time later, I read in the *The San Bernardino Sun* that he (and his newlywed wife) had been incarcerated for defying a Judge's order—actually getting married on a "high wire." This unfortunately took place at Nevada's massive Hoover Dam, while trespassing on U.S. Bureau of Reclamation property!

Another headline for "Unique McPeak."

The good news about all of this is that the Cessna's brother and sister act recovered from their injuries. But in the days that followed, rumors circulated that the guy wasn't even a licensed pilot. He'd taken lessons but wasn't supposed to be flying passengers. And the bird was overweight, taking off into a relative tailwind; the list goes on.

You know how some guys are, though—he talked "Sis" into going flying with him. Then came the wind. And then the really bad decision to use the crosswind runway. Better than that long, tedious ground-taxi to the favorable runway?

I'd like to think that (after they got out of the hospital) his sister might'a sprung for a memorable tattoo for brother dear—Do you remember what it should say?

Flying The Ultra-Ripe, Blue Plastic Outhouse

Well, *Somebody* Has to Deal With It!

The groomed dirt paths winding up and down Arizona's Grand Canyon are worn down by hundreds of thousands of hooves and Vibram-soled hiking boots every year, as are the trails that wind steeply upward to California's Mount Whitney. Spectacular views are a magnet to the John Muir or the Wesley Powell in all of us. Stricken with wanderlust, we load the wagons with children and maps and head for one colorful destination after another. And what do we do when we get there? We poop!

Sooner or later, we poop. Suzy, Bobby, and Mommy too. And Barfy makes five. Now, a real chopper pilot wouldn't normally sit down to write a story about "it," but I'm not running for office and I'm not much of a spiritual advisor, neither. Just a slightly eccentric, gray-haired old chopper pilot with a lesson to tell—so here I go.

Flying out-houses around is not what I had in mind when I learned to how to hover, but if a long-line qualified chopper pilot winds up on a fire or construction contract in these parts, he or she might wanna check the fine print, Pilgrim.

Climbers along the Mount Whitney trail poop, too. The highest peak in the contiguous USA is visited by many thousands of athletic types every year, a lot of foreigners, included. And guess what? Foreigners poop, too.

Tourists form nervous, twitching lines at one primitive shelter or another and when they are finally "number one for take off," these outdoor types universally – almost each and every one of them—toss their accumulated Coke cans, Sierra Club pamphlets, baby diapers, a few unmentionables, and some Baby Ruth wrappers in there for effect. (Saves hauling it out, which they agreed to do when they signed for their hiking permits back in Lone Pine.)

So where is all this pooping leading to, my courageous editor might ask? Liftin' them barrels up into the clear blue sky with a helicopter when they're full, that's what. And with all those aforementioned hikers, this aerial solution needs to happen with great regularity. So when little Suzy finally reaches 12,000-foot Trail Camp, her rest facility will be wint-o-green fresh & Tidy-bowl clean, thanks to a few VertRef pilots like yours truly and a passel of those behind-the-scene (GS-2 and-3) ground-pounders who bravely clip their three-way barrel-clamps to a full-to-the-rim, fifty-gallon potty can for aerial transport.

Once he's hooked up and ready to fly, our vigilant GS-2 stands next to the fragrant potty can, his senses reeling. Listening intently to his Motorola, he scans the heavens for my breezy flying machine. At last he sights the Lama and keys his radio, "Please lower your swivel hook, Captain Methane, and set me free," as he chomps on a fresh stick of Wrigley's Spearmint chewing gum.

The Forest Service deals with Mount Whitney's poop problems, and the Natural Park Service deals with the Grand Canyon's. Somebody figured it out a long time ago; you simply must have a honey bucket of some kind every few miles along the trail.

Our government doesn't exactly spend a lot of money on the problem, neither. Suffices to sink five or six fence posts in the ground, bolt some corrugated sheet metal to the posts around that all-important fifty-gallon metal can. Slap a cheap, wooden seat on top, and you're done! Except for the paperwork.

On the Grand Canyon job, we went whole hog by leasing a blue plastic "John" for some of our burly construction workers. In the dog days of summer, the work crew camped 24/7 near Bright Angel Creek, well below our scenic North Rim. The NPS wisely required the contractor to provide a portable sanitary facility down yonder for our workers, who were also rumored to poop.

So once a week it was my mission to launch the chopper from the 8100-foot North Rim Helibase trailing a 125-foot line, a heavy swivel hooked to a nylon choker belt, and auger on down into the abyss. At 4500 foot MSL and around the corner to the left, there is a scenic little grotto, just upstream from where Roaring Springs gushes straight out of a hole in the sheer rock wall.

I'd glide that Lama on down there and hit the hover button, holding 'er real steady. Hovering directly over an imaginary vertical beam, I would ease the empty choker belt on down between the tree limbs and into the hands of one of our guys. Within seconds, he would signal me aloft. Levitating the slackness out of the long line, the ripe, blue unit would be choked up tight, ready for flight.

Lifting the little lever in my left hand just a tad more caused the ship's computer to spray jet fuel all over my eight hundred ponies. They obediently burst into flame, sending six French rotor blades around in irresistible circles, hoisting the crapper straight up. Taking the scenic route up to the Rim, I spotted the Porta-John fellow standing by his "Honey Wagon," and gently delivered the toxic blue bomb to his position. After the dust settled, he hosed it out and made it springtime fresh for the return trip.

And then it happened. One Monday morning, the Porta-John guy showed up for the ritual cleansing process with no blue potty chemical! He was seventy miles away from his supply, so we had to return the crapper with just a little tap water in the hold. No wint-o-green. (At least he remembered the paperwork.)

The tap water worked for a little while. During the ensuing workweek, the lonely construction workers lured in some pretty hiker babes. Lasting relationships flourished, and many feasts were consumed. Extra food was requisitioned from above. There were additional flights for fresh Florida shrimp on ice and Texas-sized rump roasts; seconds and desserts! Before long, the small gathering grew into a movement, and then the heat wave hit. Yes, my broad-minded friends, Wingo is building up to something here.

(This was before the days of dialing "911" but what transpired inside that little blue plastic building could have been the motivating force behind the invention of the 911 emergency alert system...)

I remember well the crackly radio call the next Monday morning from the ranking foreman. Mankle's voice was raspy and weak, as he awaited my first flight of the day. "Please, please bring your long line and that twenty-five-foot choker strap and fly this crapper out of here!"

As luck would have it, the Porta-John tanker was pulling into the yard when I launched. Righteously, it was the same guy who screwed up last time. Within a few minutes, I had the offensive unit flying along in formation well below and slightly behind me, bobbing around in the breeze like a big blue bass casting jig. (It was much heavier than when I flew it down there, though.)

After shutting-down the Lama upwind a-ways, I'll never forget the scene as I walked toward the spot where I had gently lowered the crapper. When I got as close as I dared—my eyes watering— the Porta-John guy fired up the tanker's heavy-duty wobble pump. He grabbed his thirty-foot-long-by six-inch-wide (clear plastic) suction hose with one hand. With the other, he crammed two; no, three extra sticks of Spearmint gum in his mouth and started chomping.

Looking my way, he had a wild expression on his face as he brazenly flung the flimsy blue door wide open. Gnashing his teeth, he bobbed his head, triggering his mirrored eye-shades to drop down off his forehead and onto his sweaty nose.

Our hero then stormed into the hold and the horrible hose began bucking and thrashing like no tomorrow.

Which brings us happily back to Mount Whitney's Trail Camp potty, and a little history: We used to fly the "honey buckets" to the Lone Pine City sewage treatment plant, but relations between the facility and the Forest Service soured over time due to those "other things" that were mixed in with the "honey." Such items frequently clogged the facility's sewage sprayer arms and the City finally said, "Thanks all the same; but from here out, you can take it elsewhere."

Exactly one year later, I was flying a desk 300 miles away when "Pat," my replacement pilot, latched onto the Scout Lake honey bucket and woppity-wopped away with it – downhill and eastbound to a distant, remote rock quarry. The quarry was the new federally approved destination to bury such items for all eternity.

Trouble was, my replacement didn't have much long line time. But he was eager to help, you see? A seasoned, middle-aged Helitac Foreman waited for "Pat" in the southwest corner of the old quarry. Finally the Lama came into view and was soon on its final approach as "Harold" calmly radioed, "Bring it to me."

Harold wore a spiffy clean GS-7 Fire fighter's outfit that was right out of the book: Leather gloves, shiny hard hat with the local Inyo Helitac emblem, your standard high-viz reflective safety vest, and plastic safety goggles.

A top-notch FM radio hung from his utility belt in a handsomely tooled leather holster. And on his feet, a dusty new pair of the preferred fire fighter's thick-soled work boots, *"Whites."* His spotless green USFS pickup idled nearby, bristling with antennae.

Squeezing the Motorola's mic-switch clipped to his fresh Forest Service shirt's epaulet, Harold coached the pilot over the ground support frequency…"Forward, down a little, that's it, keep 'er comin'." And ol' Pat was doing a really fine job…considering what little Vertical Reference time he had under his belt…up until the time the honey bucket should have come to a dead stop, and then lowered to the ground near Harold's feet.

Instead, the bucket's forward motion was not arrested and it touched down with just enough forward speed to tip the barrel over. A generous golden tsunami sloshed over the barrel's rim, overwhelming the flimsy duct-tape-and-six-mil plastic cover, nailing our unsuspecting GS-7 from the nipples on down.

I can't think of a better time to remind our readers of the daily, unseen sacrifices that our civil and public servants perform on our behalf, often without adequate credit or compensation. On that note, here's to the Porta-John Guy. And here's to Harold, and that incredibly long, uncomfortable drive he endured before finally throwing himself into the frigid Owens River.

Photo and artwork by the Author. Special effects by Dave Mittan.
Fine tuning by Tim at Empire Camera, Colton, CA.

The log loader waits patiently near Cashmere, Washington.

"TO CATCH A SMOKEJUMPER"

Brawn Overcomes Brains.

If you've ever driven Highway 199 from "Grass Pants," Oregon, to Crescent City, California, or vice-versa, you drove past "Rough and Ready Creek," and the "Rough and Ready Sawmill." Across the highway from the mill is none other than the old Siskiyou Smokejumper Base, home of the "Gobi Botanical Refuge," the "Gorge," the parachute "Loft," and the Illinois Valley Airport, not necessarily in that order.

"Siskiyou?" you ask, to which I reply, "Kalmiopsis." For 'tis the nearby Kalmiopsis Wilderness that is home to the unique and endangered flower by the same name. "Siskiyou," according to senior-jumper-turned-science-teacher Wes Brown, is a local Indian term for "bob-tailed horse." Early Oregon history records that a treasured Siskiyou was one of several horses lost in a blizzard on a nearby mountain pass, way back when.

Centuries would pass before the U. S. Forest Service began dropping "sticks" of airborne firefighters on remote lightning fires in what became known as the Siskiyou National Forest.

Citizens, if you are new to the fire-fighting scene, you soon learn that everyone speaks highly of the Smokejumper. "Jumpers" risk it all to drop out of a grumbling old Douglas DC-3, saying goodbye to relative safety, their buddies, and their ride home. As gravity tugs, two or three muscle-bound men drift to Earth (or into tall trees) miles from nowhere, wrestling with packs weighing just under 80 pounds.

Unique individuals find this kind of challenge positively irresistible. Among the Siskiyou Smokejumper alumni are astronauts, doctors, lawyers, educators, world travelers, priests, rangers, and climbers of Mount Everest.

Dependent solely upon their muscles, their "stick mates," and their radios, they redundantly put the fires out, hike to a prearranged pick-up point, and hustle back to the Base. (To gear up in time for the next drop rotation.)

Smokejumpers—in general—are elite fire fighters dressed up like Storm Troopers. Most of these tough guys have been around the fire scene for years, starting out as ground-pounders.

With at least one year's experience on the ground, the adventurous can apply for Smokejumper Training. A few candidates annually are chosen from a plethora of applicants. Actually making it through Smokejumper Qualification puts you in a very special group of people.

(You also get initiated: taped up immediately—and vigorously—for all your accomplishments. You are then tossed like a sack of potatoes into "the Gorge," a special little wide spot in the ice-cold creek that runs through what the Jumpers call the "Gobi Botanical Refuge.")

Annually, jumpers returned to the Base in late spring from nearby homes in Cave Junction, Selma, or O'Brien. Some rotated between other bases in Florida, California, and Alaska, expanding the opportunity to jump. Those with families worked year-round, the bachelors often took seasonal lay-offs and wintered in rustic settings nearby, living close to the earth.

Exclusively a male occupation for many years, the men who wore the Smokejumper insignia were typically big, and muscular. A cartoon book I illustrated while on a Siskiyou contract in 1975 depicted them as a chorus line of muscle-bound beach bums with buzz cuts, showing off like Venice Beach, California!

And in my own humble opinion, Smokejumpers are unabashed Adrenaline Junkies, subject to lapsing into pitiful fits of funkiness when there are no planes to jump out of, no fires to fight, or no one to initiate: i.e.

"Say, Steve, wasn't that your first pay check as a Smokejumper?" (Splash!) (Steve and paycheck go into the Gorge!)

"Say, Mick, wasn't that your first cup of coffee today?" (Splash!!) (Mick and cup of coffee go into the Gorge.)

So no matter how powerful, how white, how rich or how fast you thought you could run: one way or another, everyone eventually ended up in the Gorge.

Naturally, word eventually got out that my cartoons had sullied the Knights of the Freakin' Round Table. This resulted in copious raising of eyebrows and puffing out of chests. My days of staying dry were numbered.

My situation was already insecure, in that—for the first time in its history—the Siskiyou Smokejumper Base was having to share its hallowed grounds and revered stuck-wing airplane parking lot with an all-rookie U.S. Fire Service Rappel Team and their freaking Bell 212 twin-turbine helicopter. And I was the chopper pilot - or "the Flop Wing Driver," depending on who you asked.

The thing which irritated the senior-most smokejumpers was that— for the better part of two years – they had been practically begging for the appropriation of just one sewing machine. An industrial-strength-stitching machine was sorely needed in the parachute loft.

Jumpers have to maintain their own rigging, and it takes a heavy-duty sewing machine to stitch nylon harnesses together. "Budget's too tight!" They were told to 'make do with what they had.'

Then one day along comes this big, new, expensive helicopter, shattering their relative quiet with its incessant rotor noise as rappelers practiced sliding down tandem 250-foot nylon ropes into a ten foot circle near the airstrip, perhaps two-hundred feet horizontally from the Smokejumpers' office and barracks; where frowning smokejumpers hand-poked heavy needles into thick laminations of nylon webbing, as they glared through their rattling windows at the redundant "Rope Sliders."

One of the chief instigators of initiations in this brawny mob of he-men was four-foot ten-inch Allen Owen, or *Mouse*, as he was known. The smallest smokejumper, Mouse was once on the cover of Life Magazine, featured as the "Smallest U.S. Marine" in boot camp. Mouse technically looked up to everyone, but let me assure you, he was a human dynamo; he could match some mighty big men when the sweat began to pour.

He had also run some numbers through his calculator after he got wind of the average cost for one hour's practice: "Holy horse-crap." he whined. "This danged chopper makes 324 'wops' a minute, at the cost of $.25 per wop."

Fast Forward: I lay shivering in the frigid waters of the shady Gorge—half a roll of federally funded, fiberglass-reinforced tape holding my olive-drab flight suit and every fiber of my being tightly in check. The small crowd of cheering rowdies had long since withdrawn.

My pod had done virtually the same; nature's warm-blooded response called for a full retreat of reproductive tissues in order to survive the numbing Rough and Ready creek.

Several minutes earlier, the noisy, jubilant mob had ceremoniously dumped me into a foot of the coldest water south of the 45th parallel. My 29-year-old butt rested on the sandy bottom, and by straining my neck, I could take shallow sips of air amid chattering teeth and cold spasms—if I didn't make any waves.

I reflected upon the speed at which I had gone from being a dry, happy chopper pilot to a cold, wet, quaking figure, soaking in the Gobi Botanical Refuge's baptismal stream: One moment I was writing up a detailed report on my disabled, oil-covered helicopter from inside my humble Volkswagen van, the next moment the familiar motorized "Gobi cart" (golf cart) sputtered up, loaded to the nines with grinning Smokejumpers and a fresh roll of glass-tape!

Looking up from my report, a grinning Mouse materialized before my wide-open double-doors and asked, "Say, Wingo. That was your first engine-out landing here at the Gobi, wasn't it?"

Back to the Gorge: Lying motionless, I knew I'd be cut loose faster if I didn't fight it and just acted kinda pitiful. Naturally, they love it when their victims kick, thrash, and splash. Five years in the Army taught me that one must endure a certain amount of horseplay. Unbeknownst to them, I was already working on "Revenge Plan Alpha."

I knew that Mouse was covertly monitoring me. He was lingering in the brush, just beyond the reach of any potential splashes I might make; it was his job to make sure I didn't ruin their fun by drowning.

Sure 'nuff, after a few minutes, Mouse strolled over with my wallet and cowboy boots. He then rather casually dragged me by my armpits to dry ground. Using safety scissors, he cheerfully cut through the sturdy tape binding my arms, all the while engaging me in some giddy banter. This, of course, was designed to measure my intent for a watery retribution.

Barefoot except for my waterlogged white athletic socks, my wrinkled blue fingers tugged at the last remnant of tape; I gauged the distance between Mouse and me and eagerly awaited my opportunity...

So exactly what was it that transpired and caused my Fruit of the Looms to soak up the frigid waters of the Gobi Botanical Refuge, you ask?

Well, there I was, flying that beautiful flop-wing...er...helicopter, high over the Asbestos National Forest. Carrying a full load of Rappellers and jet fuel, I held a wide orbit 2000 feet over York Peak—about to start our descent to a "heli-spot" brush-clearing mission. 'Busy work,' since there were no fires.

While scanning the gauges like any good pilot methodically does, my beady green eyes came to the No. 1 engine's oil pressure gauge. The needle dropped to zero! Stifling a knee-jerk reaction, I said to myself, 'Well, if that's true, I'll be getting a Master Caution light about now. And true to form, there came the light, proof enough that one of my turbines was cookin' with no oil in the pan!

Alerting Larry Godwin, our onboard Crew Manager, I rolled the number one turbine's throttle shut, securing the appropriate switches as I eased the cyclic back to the required 55 knots and made the radio call: "Dispatch, this is Six-Three-Six, reporting loss of oil pressure on No. 1 turbine. Returning to airport, single-engine."

Larry was isolated behind the crew seat with his six-man team. I assured him that the 212 would fly just fine on No.2, but at 55 knots, it looked more like we were hovering. Enroute, I advised the airport of our situation: "We'll have to make a run-on landing; single-engine performance will not allow us sufficient power to terminate at a hover. May need assistance."

The radio crackled with activity and I visualized a dozen lethargic Smokejumpers-turned-Crash-Rescue-Team as the word spread and The Brawn raced for fire extinguishers!

On our hot, shallow final approach, I had Larry look over the bench seat and call out the No. 2 engine's "T.O.T." (turbine outlet temp) so I could power up without having to scan the panel, allowing me to concentrate on nailing a smooth 30-knot touchdown, an improvised Head-Up Display.

Larry anxiously watched the panel as I pulled power. He keyed his headset, announcing "high green, mid-yellow, red-line" just as the skids met the asphalt. I slowly eased the collective pitch down as N59636 slid and scraped noisily down the runway to a smoky stop adjacent to the impromptu rescue unit.

Once the whooping and backslapping died down, Larry and his six rappellers de-planed and I was able to hover to the helipad and do the shutdown. Gawkers observed several quarts of synthetic turbine oil covering the left side and tail boom of the helicopter.

Maintenance quickly discovered that a chafing oil line was the cause of the problem. A new oil line was flown in, and the ship was returned to service the next day.

Cut to the Chase. I was pleased to observe that my flight suit was still dripping wet as I lunged for Mouse. "Revenge Plan Alpha" called for plenty of wet hugs for the instigator, the pleasure of transferring some of that ice-cold Gobi water on to his clean white cotton T-shirt. Mouse took off running.

As my Cherokee-bred thigh muscles kicked in, my ground speed increased; the wind was beginning to whistle past my ears. Mouse's little legs were all a-blur and his be-spackled little head was almost within reach of my outstretched Okie fingertips.

Revenge Plan Alpha predicted that we would soon be rolling in the brush and mud, along with his shiny, bloused-up Whites. Those famous, heavy-soled Smokejumper fire-fighting boots, in which he was beginning to pull away from me.

It was my danged socks that let me down, sports fans! At warp speed, the heavy wet toes began to pull away from my speedy feet, rapidly elongating into awkwardly-flapping clown-socks. Mouse left me in my pitiful tracks.

There were some hoots and manly snorting sounds coming from the mess hall window as I sloshed back toward the Gorge to retrieve my possibles. So how does one catch a Smokejumper, one might ask?

That would be *Revenge Plan Bravo.*

Photo by Doug Beck - 1975

Author (second from left) with the Siskiyou National Forest Rappel Crew near Cave Junction, Oregon and Evergreen's Bell 212 helicopter.

BLUE GUYS

Never Did Hear No Cadaver Gripe About Nothin'.

The High Sierra compares nicely to the Swiss Alps, if you ask the right mountain climber—so it comes as no surprise that Europeans flock to the good ol' U.S. of A. to climb our toughest peaks. Central California's "Alps" would certainly include the 14,240-foot granite ribbon that towers over the awesome Palisade Glacier.

Distant Mount Whitney is actually a little higher, but grandmothers hike to the top of Mt. Whitney, for cryin' out loud. The Palisades? Some of the finest Class Five climbing along the Pacific Crest Trail, they say. Yodelin' country-par-excellence! But out of respect, there'd be no yodeling this day. A climber was down. Our SA-315B helicopter would be his ride to the morgue. We averaged three or four a year.

Our first destination was the Glacier, several miles west of the Paiute-Shoshone Indian Reservation town of Big Pine, California. A fine, century-old guest Lodge near the Glacier trailhead is the staging area for those who come to scale The Chute. A small, Four Star restaurant serves fine dinners to the unfortunate few who challenge the Chute on the way up to the "U Notch," but wind up their return trip horizontal in a helicopter's basket. They're referred to as "blue guys" by some mountain rescue units.

I got a little frustrated trying set the helicopter down on the 12,000-foot glacier's surface. Whenever the uphill skid touched, the ship's fussy rotor system started to buck. The thick river of ice we were waltzing on sloped more than she liked, and the Lama preferred to buck and slide. If I got both skids down despite the bucking, she started sliding sideways, downhill.

Harold Brown and the guys did a good job of acting unconcerned, but they were holding on to their seat bottoms with both hands, I noticed.

Finally, I spotted a horizontal groove in the ice that married up nicely with the uphill skid shoe. Easing her weight onto the ice, my articulated French rotors quit their bitchin'. In the interest of safety, I had the crew climb out and move to the front. Only then was it prudent to gently split the needles and kill the shrieking engine.

Easy does it on the rotor brake, too—I didn't wanna pop out of the crack! It would be a long way to slide, and there wouldn't be enough time to re-light the engine and engage the rotors. Not a lovely thought.

Not a lovely mission, neither. My three passengers were dispatched in the early afternoon out of Independence, in the Owens Valley. We were part of the USFS Inyo Helitac crew designated "525," and our mission was to retrieve yet another blue guy.

A fellow human being (a Norwegian gentleman, we were told) had the misfortune of falling to his death while negotiating The Chute: A deep crevasse at the base of The Chute collects all who fall while scaling upward—or in his case, cascading downward.

Choosing to climb alone, he—for some reason—left his ropes secured to his pack, along with his crampons. Nearby climbers reported that he first lost his footing, finally his grip. It was a rude rocket slide straight down from that point, accelerating onto the icy apron below.

At that point, the vertical ice flared outward, guiding the unrestrained adventurer straight into the hideous, yawning crevasse at warp speed. Invariably, pink people turn blue after spending the night in the terrible hole. The unflattering tint is permanent.

I absorbed the incredible view as my silent crew emptied the Lama's external basket. Pinnacles south and west of us formed a long, jagged, razor-edged granite crown that raked the dark blue sky above our steep, slippery glacier. A large permanent snowfield on the east-facing shelf above us was the only other thing in view that wasn't vertical. A person needs dark sunglasses up here!

Looking up the sloping glacier toward the Chute, Harold dialed up the China Lake Rescue Unit on his FM portable. China Lake's small crew had hiked in at dawn to assist law enforcement with the grim extraction process, and bag the deceased. "We've got the litter secured, Two-Three, heading for the chopper," came the reply.

We could make out their distant bulky figures in the eerie flat light, pulling a covered load: the litter-sled. Our crew headed uphill to assist the tired China Lake hands.

An hour or so later, the red-cheeked Team Leader was kneeling near the chopper, briefing Harold. The fall appeared to be accidental. They interviewed a few witnesses, some who were back climbing this morning. They had quite a time hoisting the body up from the depths by hand, and were glad we landed relatively close by. After a bit more jawboning and the usual standing-around, there was finally one last thing to do: "Sign here, please," the man said to Harold, producing an official-looking form.

As the afternoon shadows lengthened, it was our turn to take custody of the blue man. He didn't object to riding in the basket. He had no luggage to check. There was no boarding pass to rip. There was no safety briefing, and we fastened his belts (tightly) for him. No coffee was served, with no cream and no sugar. No blankets were passed out, and he never did hit the red "call button" even once on the long, slow flight down to the Bishop heliport.

It felt good to leave the frigid air behind and rotor back into the waning sunshine. Harold and I were both staring at our panel's timepiece upon landing in Bishop. The sun was about to set on the High Sierra.

As soon as the rotors swished to a halt, up strode a tall figure in a white lab coat. One of those forensic fellows. Harold climbed out and pulled off his white Helitac helmet, from which he produced the familiar form—now kind of bowl-shaped and oily. "Sign here, please," he stated politely, offering the use of his standard black U.S. Government ballpoint pen.

While the responsibility changed hands, our blue passenger silently endured a bumpy transfer from the crude basket to the white sheet-covered gurney, and I was getting antsy. I was wondering to myself how on Earth we were going to fly fifty miles to Independence in time to beat the dreaded Skids-on-the-Ground deadline. The Forest Service had no sense of humor about that rule, which is calculated to the precise minute in a highly regarded USFS bible of one kind or another.

I knew what Harold was thinking: 'Damned if we're going to motel-it in Bishop, again.' To save weight, no one had packed their usual overnight gear. So before you could say *rigor mortis*, we were fired up and headed south.

Harold radioed our intentions to Dispatch as we climbed to cruise over the Owens River Valley. We could tell by her tone that the no-nonsense lady behind the mike didn't think we could make Independence in the allotted time. Harold thought we could, and so did I. At least, it would be close.

"Damn the Dispatcher, full speed ahead!"

Anyone with any 315B time in his logbook knows how slow the helicopter is, especially if you're in a hurry! The airspeed needle was teasing the 108-knot VNE mark and we were all leaning forward in our seats. That seemed to help, at least spiritually. Calling in our position every fifteen minutes as required, we couldn't help but glance at Mickey's big hand as it crept closer and closer to the "6," at which time the Lama would turn into a pumpkin.

Halfway through the flight, we realized we were going to need another ten minutes to be "legal." Sure, there was enough daylight for an emergency landing, but that wasn't the point. The Rule is the Law, and that was that. And since we couldn't speed up our Lama, we'd have to speed up our position reports! Harold got right on it.

Looking ahead ten minutes on his map, he called in: "Dispatch, 5-2-5 at Fish Hatchery Road." After a pregnant pause, the Dispatcher acknowledged. But her tone said, "lies!"

Sure enough, ten minutes out, Mickey's big hand reached the "6," and Harold's nose was growing longer and longer as he radioed, "Dispatch, 5-2-5 landing, Independence Base." The rest of us were grinning feebly and we crossed our fingers, wondering if the old gal would be checking up on us by remote control? Little did we know, the telephone was already ringing in the Helitac Shack, and there would no one to answer it for another ten minutes. We could almost hear her snicker.

And?

We didn't get away with our little deception, darn it! Coming in late earned us the dreaded Incident Report. Our vaunted mountain rescue team would be spackled up there with the dumb and dumbers in the next Regional Report, for all to see.

Sheesh! Now _WE_ were the blue guys!

Trouble at Dead Horse Pass

She was tango uniform, stretched tight—and ready to pop!

The seagoing overnight ferry to Mazatlán out of La Páz woke me up to the fact that you either pay for a little comfort on these double-decked, car-carrying rigs—or you suffer out on the deck with the rest of humanity. Long before the coastline of Sinalóa appeared in the early dawn, yours truly was among a handful of wet, shivering Homosapiens resigned to a soggy crossing on the noisy deck near the ship's stern.

There was one other gringo on the manifest that evening. "Matt" was a middle-aged freelance writer from San Francisco who eventually engaged me in some meaningful dialog, once we found the common frequency. A seasoned vagabond, he was wise to a warm area on the otherwise cold steel deck where a primate could lie prone and fight off hypothermia. I promptly excused myself and claimed a small chunk of it with my gray wool army blanket. My energy reserve was running on fumes. The familiar gray blanket smelled like Lourdes, drawing me closer. I gratefully assumed the horizontal. Sleep would come much, much later.

Underneath us that long, cold evening, massive diesel engines pounded oil into electricity, inadvertently heating the engine room's ceiling—which was our floor. That was the good part; the bad part was an out-of-balance drive shaft leading to one of the ferry's two huge screws that shook like the devil somewhere aft of us—throughout the night—a worrisome mechanical drama for any helicopter pilot to endure—reminding me of all the money I was saving. Twenty bucks. Sheesh!

At least the Dramamine was free. El Gringo Wingo was first in line following the Captain's tardy, sonorous announcement. I felt mighty green, reaching out for the pastilla offered by a grinning, white-smocked Latino sailor in a chef's hat. His hand moved just out of reach of mine, first to the left, then back to the right. He was messin' with me, I knew. One of the few daily highs this poor devil enjoyed. It was poquito embarrassing for a grown man to be brought to his knees by motion sickness. My weak-kneed inner ear had done it to me again.

Moments later, with a clammy, two-handed death grip on the nearest brass handrail, I watched helplessly: The greasy galley waxed into a queasy valley as we pounded the rollers off Cerralvo Island. Making my way to the outside rail, any romantic notion of becoming an ocean-going sailor was ejected, along with the bitter Dramamine, into the darkening Pacific. "You should have taken it an hour ago," Matt kibitzed—from the upwind rail.

It was "live and learn," on this trip. My pretty Mexican bride and I had driven down the long, torturous "Baja" peninsula highway from Tijuana to La Paz. Robertito was only four, so the three of us pulled over and slept as needed in our pickup camper's king-sized bed. The old Baja California road was a disaster that year; floods had made the going slow and uncertain. It was reassuring to have four-wheel drive for the washed-out arroyos that we forded; old "Eldo's" overload springs took on the bumps and fed them right back to us carbon-based life forms.

Lourdes had family in Mazatlán and Culiacán, but we'd never driven the Baja to get to the mainland before; something that an open-minded, mixed-race couple might have on their culture-sharing Do-List. It is not the kind of trip you'd want to make in a hurry. (Heck, I haven't been back since—except by helicopter.)

Three days after setting out, La Páz was ours. We arrived believing we would simply pay our fare and drive right up the ramp through them big, yawning ferryboat doors—and we'd soon be sailin' east.

Something was lost in translation. Our lively travel agent had been most reassuring, but there was immediately a glaring problem with our truck's California registration. A lien holder shared my pink slip, a US Bank. We needed the Bank's written permission to enter the Interior—notarized, of course. Ah, yes—the Interior...the point beyond which the casual tourist treads, and a traveler's ambitions become an interest to La Migra—Immigration.

I realized that this was something an honest man could handle by himself in a couple of days, so I offered to drive Lourdes and little Robertito to the Aero Puerto. Why hang with the gringo when they could be home with Momma Celia in two hours? Fortunately, the two were able to hop on the current big aluminum tube about to wing eastward to Culiacán, leaving Daddy behind to deal with the truck.

Two idle days went by, while I consumed *Lonesome Dove* and snoozed with the tailgate propped open, facing the beach. Baja's mild January weather convinced me that a guy could quickly get used to this latitude.

The documentation that the Federales sought materialized the next morning, and off I motored to the barco grande. When I paid my fare, the uniformed officer at the ferry's Oficina dropped another bomb on me, while counting-out my Pesos: I had planned on snuggling up overnight in the Power Wagon as the ship sailed to the port of Mazatlán—snoozing on that comfortable, custom-built foam bed I'd grown so fond of as a commercial helicopter gypsy.

"Noooo, Señor," leered the hard-eyed, mustachioed official, "No se puede." No-can-do, he was telling me…scores of vehicles were parked below in the large, unheated hold of the ship—which fills with toxic diesel fumes! No one was allowed to stay in his or her rigs. And because my hallucinating travel agent had stated emphatically that we needed no cabin or reservation, I slept on the cold, wet deck that evening like an idiot.

With dawn came hot coffee, the first thing my stomach could handle in hours. Matt joined me in the coffee line and I began to feel alive again. As we prowled leisurely around the ship, I could finally enjoy the cruise without the torment of nausea. Dolphins appeared here and there, racing and leaping to keep up with us. Several white albatrosses and brown pelicans jockeyed for position as someone in the galley tossed some cardboard boxes— heaping with who-knows-what— into the salt spray from an open door close to the waterline. We were making around twenty knots, I judged, as the gulls disappeared into our roiling wake, fussing and fighting over the sinking scraps.

Finally, the Port of Mazatlán welcomed us with a golden eldorado sunrise, and we waxed philosophical. Matt discussed his plan to barter with one of the many commercial fishing boats in the local fleet, perhaps add a good Marlin fishing adventure to his dossier. Not exactly "Islands in the Stream," but close enough. We said our cheery good-byes and I shuffled on down the gangplank to retrieve my rig.

Getting off the boat was far less a hassle than getting on—I was delighted to note—as several animated Mexican stevedores had Eldo moving down the ramp in short order. This was a sizeable logistical ordeal that the ship's crew executed with remarkable efficiency. If any of the numerous vehicles stalled, a team quickly assembled and pushed it out past the huge doors, down the ramp, and off to one side. There was another wide, deep line of rigs waiting to board for the trip back to La Páz.

Unlocking the camper shell's horizontally hinged rear door, I was relieved to note that everything was as I had left it, including my shiny new Sears toolbox. I had lost some sleep worrying about thieves in the hold, needlessly. No ratones on this boat!

Waving *adios* to Matt as he strolled toward the malecón, I drove out the harbor gates and made for old highway 15. My rust-colored pickup's 318 CID V-8 engine seemed to run well on petroleo Pemex—the nationalized gasoline monopoly—but I knew better than buying the lowest grade of gas. *Extra* cost a few more Pesos than *Nova*, but I sure didn't want the cheap stuff plugging up my carburetor jets. Something to do with lacquer accumulation, I had read somewhere.

As Eldo's customized dual-exhaust glass packs throbbed, I navigated north toward Culiacán. The flatness of coastal Sinalóa slowly turned to rolling hills. The long road ahead was an ancient, narrow, north-south motor-route. Heavily traveled, I knew the road could be dangerous, with few shoulders to pull onto if there was a problem. Which is no problem if there is no problem, but I was about to have one.

Now, Chrysler made an okay pickup in the seventies, but any decent automotive mechanic of the era could tell you at least one horror story about Mopar's poorly designed, baked-enamel ignition component that failed under the hoods of thousands upon thousands of Dodges, leaving their drivers stranded. Eldo fried one every twelve months or so. When the present resistor went south, the engine died immediately, and I ceased rumbling northward.

Fortunately—for the way things turned out—the engine's complete loss of power occurred at sixty miles per hour—just as the rig was starting down a steep hill. Shifting quickly to neutral, I was struck by the simultaneous realization that (a) I was in deep mechanical doo-doo, and (b), that I might be able to coast to the top of the next hill. The latter was a better prospect than losing momentum and parking at the bottom—or worse—on the steep upslope – a terrible configuration in which to do maintenance.

And yet, as the Dodge's momentum carried her quietly but surely toward the top of the hill, I spied something ahead that was already occupying the right shoulder. There was a peculiar, dark cloud of some sort, swirling over whatever it was—a cloud that shifted and reversed with the breeze off the ocean. It was a massive cloud of blow-flies.

Standing stiff-legged on the now powerless hydraulic brakes, yours truly brought Eldo to a reluctant, groaning halt, forty-odd feet short of the ripening biomass: A fully grown, chestnut mare lay in repose, tango uniform—teats up in the afternoon sun—her legs splayed apart at an angle the experienced traveler identified with time bomb. The umpteenth four-legged victim of vehicular mayhem along Highway 15 had come close to being detonated by my front license plate.

Whew! *That was close*, I thought to myself. A breeze blew from left to right—a darned good thing—because the truck was parked ninety degrees crosswind to the debilitating swarm-and-stench.

I had another real problem though; this was the age before cell phones or OnStar. I needed to get my truck back on the road as soon as possible. Bad things were reported to happen to travelers marooned along this old stretch of road during the night, and I wanted no part of them.

Heavy cargo trucks roared by relentlessly just to my left, as I waited to open my door and assess the ignition problem. In due time, I had my new Sears toolbox out, grabbed the appropriate socket, and backed-out a spark plug. With the hood up and the plug rigged for a one-man spark check, I turned the key: The engine cranked, but no spark! Another dead ignition component; and Captain Dramamine carried no spare!

Reassessing my dilemma, I realized how fortunate I was not to be parked any closer to the putrid pony. It was also in my favor that the year and model of my truck was very common in Sinalóa; there had to be a plethora of ignition components somewhere around here—even on a Sunday! And, yes, there was enough daylight left that—if I got real lucky, I wouldn't have to spend the night listening (and smelling) as Nature recycled the moldering mare.

Lady luck shined upon me, however: I locked the toolbox away and checked the ice covering four very cold bottles of the local Pacifico beer in the adjacent cooler. Mighty inviting! But before I could pop a top, a newish looking motor home pulled slowly up beside me during a long break in traffic. Two retired Good Samaritans had come upon a fellow human in distress.

As their door swung open, the cold blast of efficient air-conditioning hit me like a freight train. I tipped my cap towards the well-attired couple and said, "Thanks for stoppin'!" Skipping the standard formalities, the driver pointed his free hand up the hill; the pair chimed in unison: "That horse is about to pop!"

"That's very true, I'm sure," I chuckled. Climbing in, I asked the pair if they would kindly give me a ride up the road aways where fellow traveler might locate a mecánico. The couple was most agreeable and in no hurry at all, it turns out.

As the Good Samaritan drove slowly by the stiff steed, the westernmost wing of the fly swarm hammered the camper's shell like tiny hailstones. We got ourselves a close-up look at the horse-with-no-remorse. The three of us voluntarily ceased inhaling, and muttered in unison, "Eeee-youuu!!!"

Several miles to the north, a battered concrete road sign said something about a small beach community several "klicks" to the west. The Good Samaritans insisted on taking me far enough to find help, so westward we went. In a few minutes, we drove into a tiny village with no visible services. But they did have a busy (dirt) baseball diamond. The whole town had turned out for the big Sunday afternoon ballgame.

What luck! The town's "best mechanic" was the star hurler and had just finished up a double-header. And indeed, that was his 4x4 Dodge pickup parked behind the chicken wire backstop.

"Rogelio" was patient with my crude Spanish; all he really needed to see was the blistered ignition component that I dug out of my daypack. "Claro," he reassured me in Spanish, "I have one of these on the shelf."

As my Good Samaritans honked and waved adios— heading back toward the main highway— Rogelio and three of the guys from his team walked across the all-dirt main street to a ramshackle shed. There were exactly three un-crowded shelves in the diminutive, dirt-floored wooden shed, and on one of them sat the precise item that I needed. Slightly used, and no box – but it looked mighty good to me.

Within minutes, we were speeding back to "dead horse pass" in Rogelio's rig, elbow to elbow with the grinning baseball players. The dash-mounted radio was blasting out *musica de la Frontera*, punctuated with blaring tubas and mariachi-style trumpets – real tequila drinking music.

It was eighteen miles back to the pass, and though I used up all of my Spanish adjectives to prepare my crew for the mare who didn't care, they were still very impressed. Rolling by her straining, bloated hide in slow motion, my rescue team ooh'd and aah'd as the sun's low-angled rays cast four giant, field-goal-sized horsy leg-shadows onto the broken rock escarpment behind her. The larger flies also cast bizarre shadows. To a man we held our breath until we reached my truck, fearful that the slightest fart might set her off.

It only took a second to unlock the camper, grab the toolbox, and test Rogelio's "new" component. Immediately the "test" spark plug came alive, and I happily paid Rogelio the eighteen dollars he requested. We both knew that this was well below the going rate for his services—much less the ignition component—but sending them off with four ice cold Pacificos had them thanking me, as they spun 'round and headed home—their windows rolling up hastily as they accelerated through the swarm and the stench.

I set my shiny toolbox down in front of the truck's left front wheel and propped the top open. Making quick work of securing the new unit to the firewall with the appropriate sheet metal screws, I replaced the spark plug and returned my tools to the box.

There were no surprises as I swung back inside the cab and fired the melodious 318 back to life. Happily latching Eldo's hood closed, I stopped only long enough to grin and shake my head, realizing what a lucky guy I was to have escaped the Wrath of Sea Biscuit. Pulling the gear selector down to drive, I hollered out the open window, "Hasta luego, stinky!" and hit the gas.

The mare's horse-spirit must have nickered loudly as my left front tire crushed the living crap out of my new Sears toolbox-turned-wheel chock, bringing my exit to a rude halt.

And One That Got Away

Lying in the debris, I watched helplessly as they turned and left me.

One of the truly cool things about being a chopper pilot is sharing your love of flying with the public, especially the kids. It doesn't happen very often, but every now and then it just comes together, and some lucky young boy or girl gets to sit in the pilot's seat, talk to a real live helicopter pilot, and maybe go for a ride. I'm here to tell you about a time it all backfired.

Window Rock, Arizona has a nice long runway, something all pilots appreciate at 6800-feet above sea level. The Bureau of Indian Affairs painted an "H" just off the north end of that runway for Western's spiffy little MD 500D. On Day One of our little summer fire contract, everything had been signed off; the All-Navajo crew had been in orientation meetings the whole day and were now headed back to the teepee.

With camera in hand, I decided to let that golden sunset perk for a few more minutes, and then I'd wrap up the ship and head for the barn, myself. Meanwhile I turned my attention to the "injured" plastic on the ship's right front door—which had passed inspection—but the clear plastic tape we used to keep the fresh-air-vent-hole in flying condition required a new tape job above ambient temperatures of ninety degrees or so.

The area around the vent hole had recently cracked out, but we delayed the inevitable, expensive replacement with some of Scotch's toughest clear packaging tape. Satisfied that it was good for another flight, I gently latched the door shut.

Reaching into my pack, I pulled out a brand-spankin' new pair of Nikes and began tugging off my hot ol' cowboy boots as the sun and some well-positioned clouds transmogrified into a golden finale.

While kneeling to lace up those pristine sneakers, I noticed a young fella around the age of five, or so, come walking hand in hand with his mommy toward the helicopter. She was looking down the road aways. He was looking straight at me. I smiled at the expectation of making this kid's day, and put Mr. Nikon aside; denying Senior Kodachrome the image of a rare swirling bit of glory taking place behind me. Standing up next to the aforementioned door, I grinned my best grin and spoke first as mother and son approached.

"Hello young fella, ready to go flyin'?"

.......but mommy didn't seem to be in the mood. She strode right by Captain Methane and his Magical Mystery Ship and did not slow down! The path she was on headed south, paralleling the runway. Where I should be headed to shoot that killer sunset. Little Fella looked my way but didn't put up a fuss—he kept his legs churning to keep pace with mommy.

Suddenly the woman stopped, managing the little fella's momentum with ease as she turned on a dime, looked my way, and asked rather brusquely, "Why? Are you a pilot?"

I stood tall, chin up and filled my shirt with air, then folded my arms proudly. And in my best impersonation of a young Kirk Douglas, I was about to say something truly clever when I realized that my tacky tennis' toes were entangled, and I was losing my balance.

I had already committed my backside to leaning gently up against my flying machine (as I delivered said clever comeback) and I began falling backwards, my right toe locked behind my left heel. (Cue the imploding bubble door sound byte, somebody.)

* * *

The gold was lilting off the sunset, I noticed. There's a big grease blob on the overhead plastic, I'll get that later. I don't believe I'm cut, but I'm in no hurry to move, neither. Guess I could unlock my defiant arms now, and since the good woman isn't coming back to pull me out of this bed of razors, I'll have to somehow gingerly unwrap my tangled toes and levitate my sorry hide up out of this embarrassing mess, myself.

The disbelievers were well down the golden path by the time I made it to the pay-phone. Dialing the lengthy charge-card number, I realized I'd let one get away. Poor kid, I lamented, he'll probably grow up to be an airplane pilot!

"Hello, Pete?" I whimpered. "We need a new door."

Helicopter Loggers' Glossary

With my apologies to the ladies, in advance...

Abort – To terminate a turn: Stop pulling, set it down, and move on. "The pilot aborted Fatty's overweight turn and flew to Jeffro for a backup." Slang for an ugly mess.

Air Bobs – Winter work boots that have treads but no corks, or spikes. "Hey Rookie, you're gonna bust your butt wearin' them Air Bobs to work."

ALF – abbrev. for A Logging Fool.

AOG – abbrev. for Aircraft On Ground.

Backup – A turn or load of logs made quickly available, out of sequence. See turn. Hooker's Rule Number One: Always have a backup.

Bar – The long metal arm of a chain-saw, around which the cutting chain orbits in the process of cutting wood. Also: A logger's watering hole, of course.

Bar oil – Heavy, black oil used to lubricate gas-powered chain saws during long cuts. Cutters in bear country know that bears drink any bar oil jugs left in the woods!

Bar Tool – A cheap wrench that comes with every new chain saw to perform basic chain-saw maintenance, such as removing the spark plug and adjusting tension on the chain. Tool doubles as a socket wrench and a screwdriver.

Barber-chair – An unpopular way of falling a tree that tears the holding wood, making for an unsightly stump. "The Rookie barber-chaired another one!"

Beater – Any vehicle that is on its last legs. (i.e., "Kenney-Bob pushed Crash's beater into the lake and took off running!")

Bell – The heavy, sliding iron "catch" on the choker, into which goes the "nubbin." (Proper name: Bardon hook.)

Bendable buddies – Another name for chokers.

Big eye – A mythical ailment afflicting the poor hooker who keeps sending out heavy or overweight turns. i.e. with a big eye, things look smaller than they are. "Sorry Captain," Alf radioed the departing (hammered) chopper. "Guess I got the big eye this mornin'."

Bird-caged – A damaged wire rope (i.e., choker) that has been permanently tweaked into the bulging form of a birdcage.

Bite me! – Popular comeback from someone who might be lookin' for a fight.

Blob – Term used for a bright ribbon marker tossed by hookers to mark choker drops, etc. Blobs are made up by hand and hookers get mad when pilots drop chokers on their "blobs," which destroys them – especially in cold weather. (Also known as "Whoopee," "Bob," or "Roberta.")

Blow-down – The result of a storm's microburst (or a volcano) knocking down a stand of trees. Blow-down sales are the absolute worst for cutters and heli-loggers.

B'low me! – A contraction of "below me," as used in describing to the pilot where one's chokers are to be delivered. "Blow me with them chokers, Captain," radioed Big Dave, pointing toward his blob. Also: A quick way to order up a knuckle sandwich when some big feller walks by.

BLT – "Bonus, Lonus, Tronus," (or) "Boner, Loner, Troner," names meaning a six-log turn employing three chokers. (Best said through the nose, Okie style.)

Blue-haired bitch – An unpleasant logging experience. "This reprod strip is a blue-haired bitch!" (Loggers of Hispanic descent may be heard to say puta madre, which is the ultimate insult in their colorful language, so be real careful with that one; them's fightin' words.)

Blue line – Marks the borders of the Sale. Marks trees to be cut. In some sales, blue paint around the butt indicates, "leave standing," and red indicates cut. (The Seller expects the Cutter Boss to remember which is which.)

Bonus – Two logs choked by one wire rope choker. Also, "Boner, Double Boner," etc. Brush fit – A temper tantrum made worse by heavy brush, bugs, mechanical failures, etc. Bubber – Nickname for your fellow man (from the Southern endearment, "Bubba.") Buck – To saw a log cross-grain into specified lengths. Also: Chain saws can buck, and kick-back at the operator. A chain brake may prevent injury in such cases.

Buckle – To collapse, to fold. ("I knew that rookie'd buckle on us!")

Buckle-up – To stand up to. Confront a troublemaker. ("I got buckle-to-buckle w'him.")

Buckskin log – A smooth, weathered, bark-less log, usually gray in color.

Buckwheat – Pronounced "Buh-weet," a slang term for a simpleton or a rookie logger. Adapted from the character in the old *Our Gang* series.

Bug Kill – An area of the forest that has been devastated by bark beetles, etc.

Burn Sale – Salvage logging which follows a forest fire. Dirty, black, awful logging.

Butt cut – The first cut of a log above the stump. Assumed to be heavy.

Butt rot – Someone in the Crummy who needs a bath could be said to have this most preventable disposition. Also: Most common reason a butt won't pass a grade check. In older growth trees, butt rot is expected.

Carhartt – Favored brand of heavy-duty work clothing; Coveralls; Jeans.

Cat-faced – A scar on a tree formed by growing new bark around an old injury. "Drop that saw gas by yonder cat faced oak, would you pilot?" Donnie hollered.

Chaser – A rugged individual who retrieves and coils wire rope chokers as turns are delivered to the Log Landing. The chaser also stamps and paints logs headed for the mill.

Chaser Boss – The senior chaser on the log landing, also handles the ground-to-air radio.

China-eyed – A choker eye that has been stretched closed and needs to be mechanically pried open by an "eye-stretcher," a tool commonly found at the log landing.

Chokes –(Short for "chokers.")

Choker – A heavy wire rope used to encircle a log tightly when the eye-end is pulled or lifted. The average Huey choker is 30 feet in length and half inch in diameter. Some gypo-loggers use synthetic rope chokers, a practice outlawed in some forests.

Choker to stay - A hooker calls for (a "five-drop," for example) to stay when he is the second of two hookers calling for chokers simultaneously. If both drops are put on the load beam, they'll both come off together. To solve this problem and save time, the Chaser Boss will put the first hooker's drop on the hook's load beam, then thread the five-drop's stringer through the steel cage of the remote hook, where it will ride until the hooker removes it by un-belling the five drop's nubbin. (There might be a test on this later, so pay 'tension.)

Chopper – A helicopter. A meat axe. A Harley with a raked front fork, twice pipes and stuff.

Clean-up turn – When a strip gets close to being picked clean, the hooker may have to send out a partial or clean-up turn, despite good planning.

Clear! – The word to signal his pilot when the hooker is safely away from the turn and all the associated rigging, so long as the pilot takes the load out as advertised. A macho hooker will call, Clear at the hook, which means he is out of harm's way, and the pilot can immediately apply power. Also used by a pilot when hitting the starter button - a warning to stand clear of the prop or rotors.

Clear-cut – Controversial old style of logging which takes entire stands of trees down to the stump. Creates eyesores for many years to come. Helicopter logging allows for select cuts, which thins stands of trees and has minimal impact.

Clock-me-in – Term used by a chopper pilot who is searching for someone, i.e. a hooker. The hooker uses the "clock system," which places the helicopter in the center of a clock's dial, and the hooker standing on one of the numbers on the clock face. When the hooker can see the helicopter, he has the pilot turn to points on the clock, for example: "Ten and three hundred," which tells the pilot to turn left and scan the area ahead for a brightly clad fellow waving a "Whoopee." Note: Young manly types raised with digital clocks will need extra instruction! (The fastest method is to use a signal mirror, if the sun is cooperating, but not all pilots appreciate being temporarily blinded by reflected sunlight, so signal mirrors can be a nuisance if abused.) "Captain Tom pickled Tony's riggin' into the tall, dead snag."

Cluster - F_ _ k – An old military term for something that has turned into a bad joke. Also: A goat rope.

Corn-backed rattler – Field name for scat left in the woods by a homo erectus.

Corks – Caulked "shoes;" Heavy soled boots with individually replaceable spikes, made especially for loggers to be able to run around on logs. Caulks.

Corked – Stuck on one's boot. "Willy corked a corn-back rattler." Also: Deliberately kicked with a spiked boot. ("Mark corked Bildo in the face.")

Cover – A hooker who is caught short of having a turn ready asks for a "cover," whereas the pilot will opt for the closest available turn.

Cowboy – A logging pilot who takes his brain out and hands it to his frowning mechanic (holding a Bell jar) before strapping into the seat. Tosses Operator's Manual out the hole in the bubble window. Known to wear spurs.

Cranking-it-up-a-notch – A mythical step-up in turns-per-hour to keep the ground-pounders from getting lazy. It is inconceivable to the crew they might be getting slower and slower as the day drags on. There are even some who believe that sinister logging pilots can, with the flick of a switch, speed up the turn time! "Okay Loggers," bellowed Captain Methane, "I'm crankin' it up a notch!!" (Sound of a booming drum in background...)

Crummy – The designated crew transport rig for hookers, chasers, etc. [Usually the filthiest Suburban in the fleet, stinking of old rotten lunches, mildew, etc.]

Cull - A log unfit for sending to the mill, whether by rot, bend, split, twist or dimension. A choker that is worn-out. (Also, an insulting term for someone who doesn't pull his or her weight on the job. Definitely a fightin' word.)

Cutter – A sawyer or "saw;" faller or "feller." Also: A tree killer.

DSB – Abbreviation for "Deadly Sperm Buildup," the dreaded mythical disorder a manly logger develops when separated from his woman too long. "I got DSB so don't mess with me," Johnny-wad stammered.

Data Recorder – A little black box in the helicopter that computes the weight of each turn and records the daily production figures for the aircraft in terms of total weight and total turns. Other systems serve to monitor power plant and airframe exceedances. Such contraptions are unpopular with cowboy pilots.

Deadfall – An elaborate trap made out of logs that, should it fall on you - will make you dead. Originally designed by primitives to kill game or insurgents.

De-limber – A heavy, diesel-powered steel contraption that enables a loader operator to de-limb branchy logs by laying one end in a cradle and pulling the log through its two sharp, curved blades laterally, removing most of the limbs and some of the bark. Significantly reduces the workload of a knot-bumper.

Dog knot – A knot in a wire-rope choker, usually accidental in nature. Hard to undo. Knots have to be removed or the choker will eventually fail under load. "Stinky Bob, as soon as I get this half-hitch worked out of your choker, I'm comin' up the hill to thank you myself," swore the Chaser boss.

Dogs – The rigid, immobile steel teeth on a chain saw's body that dig into a log, making for faster cuts by enabling the cutter to employ more leverage during the cut.

Done – Finished, kaput; The fat lady sings; A.O.G; It's a wrap; We're suckin' mud; Throw in the towel, etc.

Doo-dah – A small log or light turn that needs to be relocated by the pilot to the closest wood patch, i.e. it won't fly with any turns on hand without going overweight. (Inefficient use of helicopter, but often necessary in thinly wooded areas.) "Hey pilot," the hooker radioed, "Doo-dah this top log to some wood b'low me and come back for a boner-loner." "Copy, doo-dah," groaned the pilot.

Drop – A choker drop, usually requested in multiples of five, i.e. "five-drop, ten-drop." A five-drop would be four coiled chokers strung by a fifth choker to the hook. (A two-drop would be one coil on a stringer, etc.)

DWB – Driving While Blind. Drunk. Pickled.

Eye – The looped and swaged end of a choker, which goes onto the lifting hook's load beam. Held open at times by means of a "thimble," swaged into place.

Eye stretcher – A simple pry-bar mechanism used to open up tight choker "eyes."

Eyeball Engineering – A quick calculation based on a visual assessment and the "Engineer's" gut feelings.

FAA – Friendly Aviators Association. "We're here to help. Now, which one of you cowboys was flying this here thing?" Also: The Tombstone Agency.

FCC – The Federal Communications Commission has their ears on, listening to helicopter loggers like they might have in *Brave New World* and Orwell's *1984*. So watch your puta madres and your X&%#@s on the radio and nobody gets hurt, see? (Freedom of speech is alive and well in the loggin' strips!)

Fat Chick Factor – A popular method of encoding heavy weights over the radio so it doesn't tend to incriminate the pilot for hauling over-weight turns, should that happen accidentally or otherwise. For example: "Four fat chicks, Willy-Jack." (A fat chick is two hundred pounds, so the pilot has just told the hooker his turn was 800 pounds overweight.)

Firewood – Seasoned cull wood, destined for the Log Landing crew to use in a warming fire or set aside for various loggers to comb through later. (Some forests are real strict about leaving it be, so heads up.)

Flash – A quick burst of sunlight directed to others (pilots, etc.) via a sighted mirror. "Hey Crash, give me a flash. I don't have you in sight." Aka *shiner*.

Flip-flop – If a log is too far from a turn to connect easily with a stringer, sometimes the hooker will request a flip-flop; whereas the pilot will lift the chokered end of the log, while keeping the other end on the ground and lay the log back down side-hill near the blob, without mashing the hooker. Release and rehook to the whole turn after the hooker collects all the loose chokers. (This is like a skid turn, only different.)

FOD – Abbrev. for Foreign Object Damage.

Forest Circus – Popular slang for the US Forest Service.

Forester – An educated, experienced and licensed forest consultant who frequently contracts out to gypo-loggers to assist in bidding contracts with federal, state or private timber sellers. Also monitors the sale during the harvest, and meets with sellers, buyers, and sawmill representatives to head off problems.

Funny – When a chaser accidentally corks a hot paint can lying near the warming Fire. It then takes off after everyone nearby, splattering everything around with hot, nasty, yellow log paint. (Best observed from a Huey, hovering high over the log landing; Pilot may have to hit the Hover Button to slap his knee!)

Fusible Link – Jokingly referring to as he or she who hooks up a log during a thunderstorm. Logging operations are normally suspended when there is a danger of lightning, around so many trees and wire rope chokers. True Story: In the dark of early morning, a preflight inspection begins on a logging helicopter that worked hard around some thunderstorms the previous day. A big, jolly, co-pilot shines his flashlight on the underside of the Bell 214's burly black rotor blade and notices a strange looking hole near the outboard tip. "What's that, Vern?" He asks his tall, thin Captain, standing nearby. Vern appraises the curious distortion to the composite airfoil and says, "That would be a lightning strike, Burl."

Goat rope – A waste of time, a wild goose chase. "What a goat rope that was." A cluster f--k.

Glitch – One of those technical problems that takes too long to explain, so everyone calls it a glitch. It's possible they can't explain it, neither, so a glitch it is. "There's a glitch in the loader's software. It just spins 'round and 'round now, like that danged helly-copter."

Goin' down – Words which are never spoken unless by the pilot and only then if he has an emergency, i.e. engine failure, drive shaft, tail rotor falls off, etc.

Grade check – Sometimes a hooker notices rot, pie cuts, etc. when a turn is reefed upward. If there is some doubt about the soundness of the wood a hooker is sending in, he'll ask for a grade check before the turn hits the log landing. "Hey Tex, gimme a grade check on that thumper comin' in - might be a pie-cut on the underside." "Copy, grade check," Tex should respond, and he'll ask the loader operator to pass judgement.

Grapple – A hydraulically powered device that allows the helicopter pilot to "log" without hookers (or chokers) in the strips. Even so, grapple logging often requires one or two hookers to "clean-up" the strips at the end of the harvest. Log loaders employ a similar grapple, which swivels.

Green spike – A yearling elk's first antler. Also, a rookie logger.

Gypo – Small scale logging operation. "Mike owned a gypo-loggin'oufit in Montana."

Hammered – Beat up; worn-out; dead tired. Machinery that has been hammered has been abused.

Hand signals – Required knowledge for all personnel working under the helicopter. [Ask your pilot for the "FAA approved hand signal portion of the Helicopter Operator's External-Load Manual."] Commit to memory.

Hardhat – Standard logger's headwear, usually painted day-glo orange. One who wears a hard hat, i.e., "You'll find him in that group of hard hats."

Hi-line logging – Traditional method of harvesting timber on irregular terrain, using a central tower powering a series of cables which drags logs along the ground. Commonly associated with clear-cut logging. Helicopter logging allows selective cutting and thinning with minimal impact on the forest and far less likely to erode later on.

Hitchhiker(s) – Debris hanging on a turn of logs that is likely to fall off. Aka riders.

Hold! – or Hold Up! – Verbal signal to the pilot during a lift to cease all movement something bad is about to happen. Applies to many problems, so have it handy. "Hold-up Captain, you're wrapped 'round a whip!"

Holding wood – A hinge of wood left uncut by the sawyer that has to be dealt with either by brute force (the helicopter) or by chain saw.

Homey – One of the local guys.

Hook – Heavy steel assembly cabled to a helicopter to entrap chokers connected to logs. A good long-line pilot is said to have a "good hook" if he doesn't smack you with it during a day's work.

Hooker – A rugged individual who works all day in the woods applying chokers to logs (turns) that are harvested by helicopter. They attach their chokers to the helicopter's heavy remote hook, which dangles from a longline well below the chopper. (Hookers break-in as chasers and are eventually promoted to hookers if they do well on the log landing.)

Hookers' Rule Book – A mythical reference manual where hookers allegedly establish reasons or excuses for doing what they just did - i.e., "Chapter three, verse ten: Never send in a loner when you can send in a boner," Byrone schmoozed the hammered pilot.

Hook rash – What hookers and chasers get if the pilot has a lousy hook. (Bruises.)

Hook shot – The ultimate slam dunk a hooker scores with one choker eye as the remote hook comes smoking in to him. Legendary hookers have been known to whip an eye onto an errant remote hook by whipping ten feet of choker sideways and scoring a direct hit. "Clear," he radios nonchalantly, it happens all the time. "Fantastic hook shot, Donnie," Captain Methane responded, his eyeballs dangling out the vent hole of his bubble window.

Hoops – Chokers; bendable buddies; chokes.

Hooter – A big log; See pumpkin; thumper; loner.

Hoot-Owl Loggin' - Working in the early morning only, when fire conditions are high. Wet bulbs help determine humidity, and when it falls below 20%, they pull the plug, choke the chicken.

Hover button – A mythical switch in the Huey's cockpit that takes over the job of hovering. "Hey pilot, hit the hover button for a second, I can't find that other eye." (Coast Guard choppers actually have one!)

Hover time – Told to the Author by a sawyer friend: "A wind logger allegedly has to work fast hooking up turns because the helicopter can only hover so long without using up all the oxygen around it - which he called *using up your hover time* - at which point the helicopter will flameout and fall out of the sky."

Hot choker – Called for when a hooker has a quick loner or boner, and no choker. The Chaser Boss will then partially uncoil a choker and send it out in the hook, saving a few seconds at the other end. A stringer would also work, if there's not a lot of limbs or tall brush overhead to lower the (trickier to control) stringer down through.

Hot hook – The remote hook gets this way when static electricity conditions prevail. Heavy rubber ("lineman's") gloves help, as do green branches or bonding wires to an electrical ground. Amperage varies, but jolts are painful; Hardcore hookers don't radio "Hot hook" warnings, on purpose. ("Let 'em find out the hard way!")

Huey – Any of a series of Bell (or Garlick) helicopters of the UH-1 series. Derived from the early Army designation, "Helicopter, Utility One, (or) HU-1."

Humphrey hump – A single log (precariously) slung horizontally from two equal-lengthed, looped chokers. (Also: Basket-sling.)

Hunky-dory – An expression implying that everything is going along just fine.

Idgit – (Slang for idiot.) An idgit is anyone foolish enough to try and catch anything (besides toilet paper) that the Captain tosses out the hole of his bubble window, i.e., rolls of orange marking ribbon, beefy rolls of duct tape, and half-full cans of orange marking paint. Every now and then, sports fans, some Golden Glove wanna-be takes on a terminal speed aerial delivery from Captain Methane with his bare hands. Broken fingers and a ton of time off usually cures 'em of that.

In the Bite – A warning to the pilot that the hooker has to stand among the logs of his out-going turn in order to attach the top choker. The pilot is obliged not to pull the slack out of any rigging until the hooker radios "Clear," as the hooker might "hang" on a taut stringer or end up under a log. "I need some steps, I'm in the bite," radioed Dirk.

Jammed – Full, maxed-out. "The log landing's jammed, pilot. Give us an hour and we'll be ready to start loggin' again."

Jury-rigged – Repaired the cheapest/easiest way possible. Chemo jury-rigged his wheelchair's parking brake with chewing gum.

Ka-Max – Kaman helicopter with two intermeshing main rotors and one pilot seat. Derived from the Kaman Husky, this workhorse will haul six thousand pounds around all day long.

Kelly hump – The odd bump or rise in a dirt road that is hazardous to lowboy trailers.

Kick out! – Term used to describe when a choker inadvertently pops out of a remote hook under tension. Time is lost in re-inserting the eye that kicked-out. This is usually caused by a loose bearing in the remote hook's load beam assembly, but worn choker eyes will shoot out of a good hook; they should be culled.

Knock-down – A standing tree taken down by the domino effect of a felled tree, or by the helicopter's load inadvertently colliding with it. The rules vary from sale to sale about harvesting the knockdown, but a stumpage fee is likely to be assessed, regardless. Think of it as a tax, if you like.

Knot-bumper – A rugged individual who finish-cuts harvested logs to the proper length while sawing off remaining limbs, pig ears, etc. Works close to the loader at the log landing. Also helps mark logs and paint the brands.

Knurled knob – A disc-shaped lever on the helicopter's remote hook which opens the hook manually, in the event its 24V power is interrupted. Used only to remove the last chokers, then the fault must be found and repaired. Manual release, aka mechanical release. The cargo hook has one, too.

Launch – To use an aggressive maneuver in getting a turn airborne. See Wenatchee snatch.

Leaner – A dangerous situation in which one tree leans into another, either over time, or as the result of a cut tree not finding a clear path to the ground. Leaners have to be ribboned-off by cutters who create them. Pilots should point them out to his busy hookers as they'll hide in the trees until the helicopter hovers overhead, when many come down with little or no provocation. "Heads-up on a leaner snag at your six o'clock, Ted." "Copy leaner," Ted should acknowledge.

Left foot, right hand – If a rookie hooker gets zapped by a hot hook, ask him if he had both his feet on the ground. Whatever he answers, instruct him to stand on his left foot and reach up for the hook with his right hand. It will eventually dawn on even the thickest skulls that that don't work, neither. (Funny, though!)

Lick nuts – Sentiments from tough PMs like Kelly Cannon when the boys ask for a couple of hours off to run into town and cash their paychecks. (He declined, in other words.) Shorter version: "Lick 'em!"

Loader – Heavy, diesel-powered rig used to manhandle harvested logs and load log trucks. Demands experience and lots of skill to operate at production speed, and occasionally gets nailed by an incoming log. Most loader operators are gorillas in hardhats. They de-limb the unfortunate helicopter pilot who hits their loader with even a small log.

Log brander – A branding iron type of tool built into a heavy hammer that the Chaser Boss or his designee swings hard at both ends of a log as soon as it hits the ground. The unique design on the brand is approved (by the USFS, for example) in advance and is examined at all scales to keep gypo loggers, mill reps, and log thieves on their toes. (If a log end is trimmed, it has to be rebranded.)

Log deck – The accumulation of harvested logs that are neatly stacked by species and length by the loader in preparation for shipment to the sawmill. (Also: Deck.)

Log landing – Where the logs are delivered by the helicopter, and where log trucks meet the loader in order to load up (50,000 pounds, usually) with timber destined for the sawmill.

Loner – One log suspended by one choker. Also: Someone inclined toward bachelorhood.

Mill – Sawmill, where logs are scaled (measured and/or weighed) and sawn to specifications.

Mo-jo – That which excites one or provides stimulus. "He's got his mo-jo workin'!"

Montana Slow Elk – A cow.

Motion lotion – Jet-fuel for the helicopter.

N.A.P.A. – What a resourceful Huey mechanic refers to as the "National Aircraft Parts Association." Often much closer than an OEM (Original Equipment Manufacturer) but not an F.A.A.-approved parts house.

Nice hook! – Compliment paid to the pilot for bringing the hook in to the hooker/chaser/etc., just right. Or, anytime the pilot doesn't drop it on your foot or smash you with it during the hook-up process. Or, anytime he does! (Sarcasm abounds over the radio.)

Nitpicker – Someone who looks for the tiniest flaw in virtually everything.

Nubbin – The end of a choker opposite the eye, which is swaged into a small knob for inserting into the sliding portion of the choker, or bell. Nubbin hooks take nubbins instead of choker-eyes. Nubbin hooks are common on Type 1 helicopters. See: Type 1 Helicopters.

Nut Buster - Words to describe anything from a bad road to a rigid suspension, or something subtle like a short-handled rake lying in the grass, waiting for a lackey to step on it wrong. "That clean-up job on Fatty Creek was a nut buster," Newt whined.

Oaklie-Doakley – Ned Flander's way of saying "Okie Dokie." It works in the woods.

One-eyed trouser snake – Slang for what a man also might refer to as his Johnson. Party Manager – the Project Manager, or P.M. Works under the owner or Logging Superintendent.

Pecker head – Somebody along the level of a buckwheat, honyocker, pie-cut, cull, etc. (More fighting words.)

Peeler – A freshly harvested log, which is peeled into sheets of veneer for paneling.

Pickle – A large single log. Also: Hooter, pumpkin, etc. Or, to drop a load of chokers, logs, etc. that is overweight or has snagged during launch.

Pie-cut – A large watermelon slice-shaped cut made in a fallen log in the process of either testing for rot or designating the log as a cull. Also: Nickname for a slacker. (Fightin' words, if said with no smile.)

Pig ear – A sharp stub of what was a branch on a log that should be sawn off flush with the log to pass the sawmill's specifications.

Pike - A metal tipped spear with a barb for maneuvering floating logs.

Piss fir – This big fir isn't known for its quality lumber, neither.

Piss test – The dreaded pre-employment, random, for-cause, and post-accident threat hanging over any logger who has been having a little too much fun.

Pitch – Sticky concentrations of natural sap in the interior wood of the random pine log, which is treasured for starting warming fires in wet conditions. Pitch burns quickly but produces a thick, black smoke. Also: Pitch log - One which renders pitch. Pitch stump.

Pounds-per-turn – or PPT: Production information helpful in evaluating how close to the goal the hooking crew is doing. The pilot determines the PPT by dividing the total weight at the end of the day by the total number of turns. Example: 650,000 pounds total weight divided by 240 turns equals 2708 ppt; which is so-so.

"Pull hard, she'll come easy" – Favorite expression for a hooker who has a demanding, heavy, tricky or impossible turn for his pilot to try.

Pumpkin – A large, heavy log; hooter; thumper. i.e. "Byron's hookin' in a pumpkin patch, and I'm jealous!" whined Jeffro.

Quad – or quadronus – Four logs suspended by one choker. Also: A one-man 4 by 4.

Rack – A set of antlers left behind in the woods. A "full rack" also describes the mammary glands of a well-endowed female of the species homo erectus.

Ramrod – The boss. The head honcho. (From the black powder days of ramming the ball, powder, and patch into a mussel loader: If your ramrod broke, your rifle was useless except for hand to hand combat.

RCH – abbrev. "Red C--t Hair," describing a very small increment or distance.

Reprod – Short for a stand of young trees, all about the same height, thirty years or so from reaching harvest size. An annoying place to be stuck in for long!

Rider – (See "Hitchhiker.") "There's a rider on that turn, pilot." "Copy rider," Hollywood acknowledged.

Riggin' – A term used to assess one's quality of work, i.e. "Nice riggin' on that Skip-and-Vern, Alf." (Also, a logger's personal equipment: "Crash, your stinkin' dog piddled on my riggin' again!" Ted shrieked.

Riggin' Fit – A temper tantrum associated with bad wood and/or chokers. "When the pilot dropped Alf's chokers into his warming fire, Alf threw a riggin' fit!" (See "Brush fit.")

Rigging slip – When chokers slide and suddenly "catch" on a choked log, giving the helicopter a "shot," or sudden jolt. (It'll knock your fillings loose!)

Rinse Cycle – The next-to-last logging cycle of the day.

Rip and Tear – Term for the extra effort that will be required to free up logs that are held down by other logs or iced-in limbs, for example. "Rip and tear!" (Or) "Let 'er rip, tater-chip." Mike Robey would always say.

Ripped – A log that has been cut in half with the grain, using a "ripping saw." Also: Slang for muscled to the max; Too stoned to move; Pickled.

Rocket Scientist – A complete freakin' idiot.

Roller! - Shouted when a log segment (butt-cut, boulder etc.) heads down the hill toward anyone. The items that roll downhill, i.e. rocks, pie-cuts, etc. Rollers.

Root rot – The deterioration of a tree's root system which can subject the tree to falling over under the rotor-wash of a low-hovering helicopter. Slang for a non-specific disease said to have affected ones' tool.

Root wad – A tree that has been blown down or knocked down and its roots are partially or completely exposed. If the root wad is to be flown to the log landing, there is the danger of rocks that are nestled in the roots from falling on personnel/equipment along the flight path. Some forests require the roots be bucked prior to flying them out, but they distinguish between knockdowns and blowdowns.

Rube Goldberg – A successful engineer who popularized complicated mechanisms performing very simple functions.

Russian – from: "Rushin'" as a cutter who didn't cut a log all the way through Because he was *in a rush*. Hookers are trained to call-out "Russian" when they observe a log in their turn being lifted that is partially cut, as it may break at a bad time and fall on personnel, equipment, and/or endanger the helicopter, therefore the hooker. (A saw may have to be flown in to finish the cut.)

S-61 – Sikorsky helicopter capable of lifting 8,000 to 10,000 pounds on the hook. Has a good logging safety record. The "61" comes in many models from the "A" to the "Shortsky." Was chosen the Presidential Helicopter for many years.

S-64 – The larger brother to the S-61. Resembles a praying mantis in flight. Known as the "Tarhe" in military circles. Includes CH-54A through S-64F models. Sack – Another word for manliness. "Newt showed a lot of sack to straddle that bull!" (Also, the anatomical location within which one's manliness is suspended; scrotum.) or to fire: "Boudreaux has been sacked," Fatty was happy to say.

Sale – The limits of a timber harvest as described in the contract; awarded as a Sale.

Saw – A gas-powered chain saw or the person who operates a saw, from "sawyer." (Also: To cut with a saw; to sleep: "He's sawing logs.")

Saw boss – The senior sawyer or cutter in a sale. All cutters work under his direction.

Scat – Mammal droppings of the larger species, i.e. bear, moose, elk, deer, lion.

Service – (or Service landing) – Where the logging helicopter is based or refueled.

Shiney (or shiner) – A signal mirror, used to direct an aircraft to the signaling party.

Short bite! — As the helicopter lifts a log, chokers sometimes tighten up at the last instant, grasping the very end of the log as it rises into the air. The hooker should call out "short bite!" to alert the pilot that he may lose the log any second. Most "short bites" ride all the way to the log landing, but those that don't create a hazard. Rigging slips of this nature can either be reset or aborted to give the hooker time to reset the choker further down on the log.

Shot – When the helicopter is subjected to a rude jolt or sudden stop, it is said to have taken a "shot." The shot usually comes from a hidden source such as a wrapped tag. Also: Broken, worn-out, useless. "Hightower's engine was shot after he drove his new 4x4 rig into high water at the quarry."

Shovel – A heavy tire or track-mounted rig used to excavate or grapple-log. Also, the equivalent of a hi-line logger's remote hook; "Drop your shovel, Pilot. I got a troner-loner for you," ol' Boudreaux used to holler.

Sissy-turn – Derogatory, for a light turn. ("Darn it, Rookie, I'm gonna start callin' you the Two Pound Clown if you don't get your weights up," growled the Woods Boss. (2,000 pounds - or "two-pounds," whereas the minimum weight of a turn is usually 2,800 pounds to 3,000 pounds, and up to 20% of that will end up in the slash pile.) (A thin profit margin keeps the pressure up!)

Show Me the Way! – Radio code used by a hooker who needs a longline hook ride for one urgent reason or another, such as, to render first aid to an injured woodsman. "I'll show you the way to the West side of the drainage," Captain Bart bellowed.

Shroomin' – Abbrev. for "mushrooming:" Spaced out on psychedelic mushrooms. They found Willy's radio and riggin' at the edge of the cow pasture, where he had inadvertently stumbled upon some little blue mushrooms.

Skid-turn – Describes the need for one log to be skidded a short distance to other logs in order to bring a lightweight turn up to weight. Seldom employed when the chopper is low on fuel or where triple-stringing will do the job.

Skip & Vern turn – A two-log turn comprised of one short, thick log and one long, skinny log; named for Skip Fisk (deceased) and Vernon Sanders, respectively. Skip and Vern were well known Bell 214 and S-61 logging pilots in the Western USA and Alaska.

Slack choker – Warning to a pilot that at least one log in the turn he is lifting has not taken the strain on its choker and may soon give him a shot!

Slack-jawed Faggot – A sordid expression originated by a certain Woods Boss who didn't care for this other feller very much and made up that prickly phrase to enrage and provoke just about anyone on Earth, sooner or later. Them be fightin'words!

Slash – Term to define piles of freshly cut tree limbs that slow a hooker down. "I'm all slashed in here, moving kinda slow, need steps," etc.

Sled – Any underpowered vehicle. A weak helicopter on a hot day. Also, a lead sled. "My sled done busted a crank out past the mill," Danny whimpered.

SNAFU – Yes, loggers use this old abbreviation frequently: "Situation Normal, All Fouled Up" (…or words to that effect.)

Snag – A standing dead tree often hazardous to loggers, due to falling limbs, etc. To catch around a tree, i.e., "Hold it Vern, you're snagged on a whip."

Snaggle-toothed Sue – (Come to think of it, let's move along.)

Snoose – Snuff. Chewing tobacco used by loggers who then squirt the juice into an empty bottle or paper cup that they usually leave rolling around on the floor of the helicopter or the Crummy. Just lovely.

Spanked – Exhausted. "Shut that *$#@&! helicopter down, pilot. We're all spanked."

Spin cycle – The last cycle of the day. "Is it the spin cycle yet?" Rosy wanted to know, applying more vagi-kream to his rash. (Sorry, ladies!)

Spread-eagled – A turn that is laid out in all directions from the pickup point.

Squaw hump – A log that a hooker can't get a choker under, requiring the pilot to pull tension on a choker looped under the downhill edge of the log in order to gently pull the log clear of its impression.

Starter turn – For a Huey, a turn that weighs between 2,500 to 3,000 pounds.

Staub – A sharp piece of a limb on a log, notorious for snagging a logger who's in a hurry. "Newt ripped his sack on a staub, Billy-Bob, and he wants you to go down yonder and help doctor it." (More fightin' words.)

Steps! – A hooker will ask the pilot for steps when he is in-the-bite, to make sure the pilot understands that the hooker is in harm's way until he calls "Clear!"

Stinger – A long aluminum boom which forces a logging trailer to negotiate sharp turns behind a diesel tractor. Stingers break now and then and spoil the whole day.

String (or strung) – Employing a choker or two to connect distant logs, i.e. double-strung, triple-strung, etc. (Also: Strung-out, as on drugs....)

Stringer – One uncoiled choker hanging from the hook, for quick turn-arounds.

Strips – Short for logging strips, or where the wood to be fallen or harvested is located.

Suckin' mud – An old well driller's term for futility. "Shut 'er down, Virgil; we're suckin' mud."

Sweet Hook – Compliment paid to pilots who bring the remote hook in just right.

Tag – A lightweight log that is designed to come up last in a multi-log turn. Tags can whip around standing trees when the turn is "launched," which is a bad thing. Different types of tags: "Chinese," "Gypsy," "Y-Tag," and "Slider." (The latter of which are outlawed in most forests for safety reasons.)

Tag-on-Tag-on-Tag – A hooker's lament for a light turn of multiple logs strung from one to the other, exceeding two hundred feet in length at times.

Tailboard – A safety meeting. Originates from the old days of gathering around the open end of a wagon with the tailboard down for a place to sit and parlez.

Tape – A cutter's measuring tape, also used by log scalers and knot-bumpers. Also: Duct tape, used by hookers to help waterproof their leggings against the weather, and to help start wet kindling for warming fires.

Thumper – A big log; a hooter; a pickle; a pumpkin.

Tight eyes! – A hooker who is barely able to pull his choker eyes together will call for a low hook when he has tight eyes, because he may not be able to reach a remote hook that is hovering over his head. If a low hook doesn't work, it becomes a pull together.

Tin pants – Heavy-duty canvas logging pants impregnated with paraffin or candle wax to help keep out the weather.

Tongs – A tool used to clamp on to a log under which the hooker cannot shove a wire rope choker, usually because the underside of the log is buried or lying on rock.

Tool – A man's unmentionable; Trouser snake; Johnson, etc.

Top – (or tops) - To cut the unmarketable dimension off the uppermost log of the tree, leaving a small "Christmas tree." The upper-most portion. Also: Old growth timber had to be "topped," to help reduce wood loss as the huge tree bends during falling. Someone has to climb to the top of the tree to fell the top, then climb down for the final cut at the stump.

Town pump – Central gas station in small town. (Also: A woman with few inhibitions.)

Trailer queen – The reigning female matriarch of a given mobile home.

Trailer trash – Those barely able to afford a mobile home. *Les Miserables*.

Tronus – Three logs suspended from one choker. Also troner.

Trouser snake – See "tool." Also: One-eyed trouser snake.

Tube steak – A hot dog.

Turn – One load of logs flown from the logging strips and delivered to the log landing. A turn can be one log or several logs that weigh-up enough to warrant harvesting.

Turns-per-hour – The pilot calculates turns per hour by dividing total turns for the day by hours flown. Example: 240 turns divided by 7.9 hours (skids up) equals 30.4 tph, or a turn coming in every two minutes.

Tutu – A ballerina's frilly lace skirt. A lightweight turn weighing 2,200 pounds. (See: Sissy-turn; Two-Pound-Clown.)

Two-bagger – A woman so ugly that, in order for you to mate with her, you must put a paper bag over her head. This is done *after* you put a bag over your dog's head, so he won't lose respect for you.

Two-Pound-Clown – A hooker who continuously falls short on the weight of his turns. See: Sissy Turn.)

Type One – A classification of large helicopters, including the Boeing Vertol, Sikorsky Sky Crane, S-61, Blackhawk, Kaman Ka-Max, etc.

Un-bell! – A verbal warning to alert the pilot lifting a turn that a log's nubbin has popped out of a choker's bell. Action stops while the hooker runs in to reset the nubbin into the choker's bell. Also, a hooker asks for an "unbell" on a single log coming into the log landing if he can use the resulting stringer on his next turn. This usually saves time, but not always. NOTE: A good hooker knows to wedge a small stick in the bell to help keep the nubbin from popping out prematurely. Takes a little more time, but saves time.

Vagi-Kream – Jokingly requested by a dead-tired hooker when he's needing a choker drop and some time to recover his strength, i.e.: "And a five-gallon jug of vagi-kream along with that ten-drop, if you got any."

Wash cycle – Three logging cycles from the end of the workday.

Weasel – A cheat. An undependable person. A mean little rat. A scumbag.

Wedge – A tough plastic tool designed to help prevent a partially cut tree from falling in the wrong direction.

Weight-abort – A turn that is too heavy to lift or too light to make weight.

Wenatchee snatch – A cowboy pilot's way of persuading a heavy log or cluster of logs off the ground by being aggressive: Keeping his extra-long, long-line taut, Cowboy's main rotors fan the uphill treetops. Holding his tail rotor control pedals stiff-legged and neutral (spurs jangling.) Cowboy launches his Huey backwards. Unloading his tail rotor this way, he allows torque to turn the helicopter 180 degrees to the right, while the logs below slowly begin to rise. Two hundred feet above them and gaining speed, Cowboy applies a well timed deflection of cyclic, which reefs the whole turn into the air and commands it to ffffollow him! (A risky maneuver, not recommended or endorsed by the author.)

Wet-drop – A radio call from a hooker requesting a plastic jug of water be sent out with his next choker drop. "Don't pickle them chokers, Joe. That's a wet-drop and I gotta water my whistle."

Whip – A small green tree or limb that interferes with logging, i.e. "Pilot, give it another yank, your tag is hung on a whip." Also: Tired – "We're all whipped."

White hats – Code name for supervisor types who commonly wear white hard hats. Also, The Overhead. "Hey guys! Look busy. A couple of *white hats* are comin' up the road in their air-conditioned Jimmy."

White rot – Wood rot that makes certain species of conifer unmarketable.

Widow maker – Any number of dangerous situations including a "hitchhiker," "leaner," or fragile dead tree top (or limb) which may fall and injure a nearby unsuspecting logger.

Wimp – A weakling. One of those "girly-men." Devoid of sack. (Fighting words!)

Wind loggers – Another name for helicopter loggers. Also: Sport loggers; Huey loggers.

Wood – Trees that have been fallen and cut to marketable length. "We got a lot of wood scaled today," Willy bragged. Also: Slang for an erection, i.e. Jeffro couldn't run very fast with a woodie, his speedy girlfriend noticed.

Woods – When you can't see the forest for the trees, look for the woods, I reckon.

Woods Boss – The boss under the Project Manager, sometimes one and the same.

Chasers and hookers work under the W.B. The W.B. is, by necessity, the biggest, toughest guy on the crew. He has to work several strong men into near-exhaustion every day through mind-numbing labor under harsh conditions. And some of these guys eventually get their fill and challenge the W.B. to a fight. (The W.B. had better win.)

Wrap – Verbal warning to a pilot during the launch of a turn, whereas a tag has inadvertently whipped (or wrapped) around a standing tree and may cause the helicopter a shot, an abort, or both. Also: End of production, "It's a wrap!"

Z-Man – My old loggin' buddy, former Marine and ace helicopter mechanic, Jerry Zirnheld. (Semper Fi, Jarhead!)

Zapped – Shocked by a hot hook during periods of high static electricity. Hit by lightning; Stoned. Pickled.

The End

CPSIA information can be obtained
at www.ICGtesting.com
Printed in the USA
FFHW021451040119
50063540-54880FF